YOU SELF-PUBLISHED, NOW WHAT?
HOW TO PROMOTE YOUR BOOK

Also by Mateja Klaric

Self-Publishing Made Easy, Book 1
How to Self-Publish Your Book:
The Fast, Free & Easy Way
2nd Editon (2018)

Self-Publishing Made Easy, Book 1
How to Self-Publish Your Book:
The Fast, Free & Easy Way
1nd Editon (2017)

The Fox & White Rabbit, Book 1
The Story of the Fox and White Rabbit
(not your ordinary fable)

YOU SELF-PUBLISHED, NOW WHAT?
HOW TO PROMOTE YOUR BOOK

Mateja Klaric

You Self-Published Now What? How to Promote Your Book
First edition, November 24, 2018, published by Mateja Klaric
Second book in the series *Self-Publishing Made Easy*
ISBN: 9781790156917

Author: Mateja Klaric
Proofreading: James Reeves
Cover & book design: Mateja Klaric

Copyright © Mateja Klaric 2018

All rights reserved. No part of this book may be used or reproduced in any manner whatsoever, including Internet use, without written permission from the author. Publications are exempt in the case of brief quotations in reviews or articles.

Dedicated to all who have stood by my side in the time of need. Thank you for your invaluable help and support.

Special thanks to James Reeves, my patron on Patreon.

TABLE OF CONTENTS

1. **WHERE TO BEGIN** 1
   - The Rule of 7 1
   - Tools of the trade 2
   - Priority list 3
   - Stay organized 4
2. **WHAT NOT TO DO** 6
   - Rule #1 - avoid wasting anyone's time 6
   - The NOT-to-do list 7
3. **MINDSET** 9
4. **THE THREE BASIC QUESTIONS** 11
5. **AUDIENCE** 12
   - Narrow it down 12
   - Audience by genre 13
6. **PLATFORM** 14
7. **BLOGGING** 15
   - Medium 16
   - Ello 18
   - Quora 19
   - Tumblr 20
   - WordPress 21
   - Patreon 22
8. **GUEST BLOGGING** 23
9. **PUBLICATIONS** 26

10. SOCIAL MEDIA 28
- Facebook.. 29
- Instagram 30
- Twitter.. 31
- LinkedIn... 31
- Google+... 32
- Pinterest 32
- Reddit.. 33

11. E-MAIL LIST OF SUBSCRIBERS...................... 34
- How to get subscribers 34
- Quality over quantity....................................... 34
- Conversion rates... 35
- Subscription forms 36
- Sending newsletters 39

12. NETWORKING & GROUPS 42
- Writers' groups & communities 42
- Street teams 43

13. FREE AUTHOR PAGES 44
- Amazon Author Central................................... 44
- Adding RSS feed 45
- Goodreads... 45
- Books2Read author page 46

14. WEBSITE, DOMAIN & EMAIL......................... 48
- Domain 49
- Hosting services and emails 50

Website builders 52

Content & design 53

15. YOUR BOOK AS A TOOL 54

Promote your other books 54

Grow your email list 54

Ask for reviews 55

Bio and links 55

16. BOOK COVER DESIGN 56

The role of a good book cover design 56

Non-fiction 58

Fiction 58

DIY cover design 59

17. BOOK DESCRIPTION 63

Blurb 63

Logline 64

Ad copy and tagline 66

Copy for book promotion sites 67

18. AUTHOR BIO 69

Byline 69

About the author 70

Author pages 70

Author website and blog 71

19. PRICE POINT 72

How to find and evaluate the data 72

Free ebook offers 74

Free ebooks on Amazon 76
20. PREORDERS 78
21. CATEGORIES & KEYWORDS 79
Categories 79
Keywords 81
22. REVIEWS 82
Readers' reviews 82
Book blog reviews 84
23. THE COST OF PROMOTION 86
24. PROFIT & LOSS 88
Creating P&L sheet 88
Estimating your book's sales 89
25. WHY BOOKS DON'T SELL 92
The buyer's journey 94
26. MEASURE THE RESULTS 97
Website and blog stats 97
Sales and author rank 98
Paid ads stats 99
27. BOOK PROMOTION SITES 104
Recommended sites 104
Policies 106
Cost 106
Results 108
Check everything twice 109
What to avoid 110

28. PAID ADS 111
Book platforms vs. social media 111
Amazon Advertising 114
BookBub Partners 119
Goodreads 121
Social media advertising................................. 122
Facebook & Instagram 123

29. AD DESIGN & COPY TIPS......................... 128
3D book mockups.. 128
Ad copy tips... 130

30. GIVEAWAYS.. 132

31. OTHER OPTIONS 134
Video trailers 134
Audiobooks 135
Online Courses 135
Merchandise.. 135

32. PROMOTION PLAN 137
Plan activities by cost 137
Plan long-term... 138

33. USEFUL APPS AND TOOLS 141
Social media management............................. 141
Design and 3D mockups 142
Free images and videos 143
Topic finders and title generators 144
Keywords and Amazon categories 144

  Book sales analytics 145
  Website tools 145
  Social media ads 146
34. FINAL WORD..147
Recommended reading 148
References..151

WHO IS THIS BOOK FOR?

This book was above all written for writers who self-publish on a budget and are not sure how to promote their books in the most affordable and cost-efficient manner. It might, however, also be useful to those who are interested in publishing with a traditional publisher.

You can promote your book in different ways, but not all options work equally well and much depends on what kind of budget you can afford to invest. To run a good book promotion campaign, you must take into consideration many other factors in addition to the budget as well, such as the genre and audience.

This introduction to book promotion will provide you with a comprehensive overview of different options available to writers. It will also show you how to start looking at everything related to writing and books as a part of marketing and promotion activities.

Book promotion is not just about paid ads. Knowing this is especially important for those who are trying to promote on a budget. Expensive approaches to book promotion remain beyond the reach of many and that's why I wrote this book – for those who could use some budget-friendly guidance.

The tools of the trade, among other things, include cover design, ads, blogging, book promotion sites, social media presence, and more. We will cover all of it. The book is written as a DIY guide that includes recommended services, apps, and tools.

WHO AM I TO WRITE IT?

In addition to self-publishing two books prior to this one and running an advertising agency for eight years, I spent my whole career working in the media. But book promotion is highly specific. It's one of the most challenging fields one can imagine, with thousands upon thousands of competitors that include both big publishers and indie scene.

While there are many areas where work experience in marketing and promotion come in handy, there are specifics to book promotion. Also, trends, rules, and apps nowadays keep changing fast, and strategies that worked yesterday might no longer work today.

There are quite a few writers who sell courses on book marketing and promotion. But even though these writers are highly successful in their genre or work, not everything they recommend will necessarily work for every writer, every book, and every time.

Book promotion is not as simple as saying, 'this worked for me, so it must work for you.' This is not necessarily so. The two books I self-published, for instance, are very different – one is a fable and the other a how-to book on self-publishing.

The same book promotion site where I promoted them worked well for one but did nothing for the other. I spent a year researching and testing various options with my books and put many of the claims to the test. While some recommendations indeed worked, others brought little or no results.

I managed to get my books to #1 in several categories on Amazon. My highest free rank among all Kindle ebooks on Amazon so far was #1,090, and the highest paid rank #11,512. I achieved this on a tiny budget – an amount Mark Dawson spends on Facebook ads per day.

In this book, I'm sharing what I have learned to help you avoid some of the pitfalls and misconceptions about book promotion. For a start, keep in mind that no serious advertising agency will ever promise their clients results.

They cannot do that because there are too many unknowns and other factors advertisers have no control over. Book promotion is no different. My first advice would thus be, beware such promises and those who make them, and second, get ready to test, test, test.

NOTE:

I am not affiliated with any of the products, platforms, and services recommended in this book. There are no affiliate links. The recommendations are based solely on sincere satisfaction with these products and services.

1. WHERE TO BEGIN

Book promotion doesn't begin after you self-published a book. It begins by building your platform and finding your audience. In other words, it begins by finding people who might be interested in buying your books well before you publish.

Writers who made it with their first self-published book are rare. Most people hate taking risks and buying a book by an unknown self-published writer is perceived as a risk. Potential readers are much more willing to take a chance if they already know the author and like their work.

That's why traditional publishers aren't interested in publishing books by writers who don't have either a following or a story that might be of interest to the media. They know that unless you already have a platform or something exceptional to share, your first book stands little chance of selling well.

You can, of course, self-publish and at the same time work on building an audience. That, however, usually means that you cannot expect to make a profit even if you invest in promotion. The book might sell, but the initial investment will be higher. One of the reasons for this is the Rule of 7.

The Rule of 7

The Rule of 7 is a well-known phenomenon in marketing and psychology – it means that a potential buyer has to see a product (or a brand) at least 7 times before he or she is ready to buy [1]. That's why book promotion isn't a short-term activity you only have to do once and then forget all about it. It's something that never ends and should begin before the book is even written.

The Rule of 7 is one of the reasons why a preorder option is worth giving a try – it will give you the time to promote and make sure people already saw the book several times before it gets published.

Tools of the trade

Here is the list of activities writers use in book promotion. This is just a basic blueprint and we will expand it with additional options later:

1. **Blogging, guest blogging, publishing in publications**
2. **Growing your email list of subscribers**
3. **Being active on social media**
4. **Joining writers' groups and networking**
5. **Creating efficient book cover design**
6. **Writing alluring blurb and book description**
7. **Using back and front matter in your books**
8. **Creating free author pages and website**
9. **Promoting on book promotion sites**
10. **Promoting with paid ads**
11. **Getting reviews**

This is just a basic list of activities, but it may already seem overwhelming. You don't have to take care of everything at once, though. Not every item on the list is of equal importance and that's why you need a priority list.

Priority list

Create your priority list and start working on first things first. The most important activities for a writer on a budget are those that can bring the greatest and most sustainable results at little or no financial cost.

But while these activities don't require a significant financial investment, they do require an investment of time and they will not lead to instant results. On the other hand, though, they are the best way of building a platform of loyal readers, and that's priceless.

Here is the suggested top priority list:

1. **Blogging, guest blogging, publishing in publications**
2. **Growing an email list of subscribers**
3. **Being active on social media**
4. **Creating efficient book cover design**
5. **Writing alluring blurb and book description**
6. **Using the front and back matter in your books**
7. **Creating free author pages**

By blogging and publishing your work in publications, growing an email list, and being active on social media, you get your work in front of the readers. That's how you find people who might be interested in buying your books.

How you present your book is also a top priority. Book cover, blurb, and book description all have the power to make or break the sales. Use the front and back matter in your books as well. Look at it as a free advertising space where you can promote your books and invite the readers to subscribe to your email list.

Finally, create your free author pages on platforms such as Amazon Author Central, Books2Read, and Goodreads. You can do most of this at no other cost than the investment of time and effort. Take care of these things first and wait with paid promotion until you have polished the book and your online presence. That's how you can maximize the results.

Stay organized

To keep track of various activities, you will have to stay organized and make plans. This is especially important when you will start running a paid promotion. You need to keep track of how much you invested and measure the results to see what worked and what didn't so that you can cut the losses fast.

It's very easy to lose track and spend too much money if you neglect that. Traditional publishers also create P&L (profit and loss) sheet for every book they publish. They use it to estimate the potential for profit and set the budget for promotion. The person in charge of the book then monitors the expenses and tracks the sales. As a self-published writer, you are this person in charge of promotion and responsible for the sales of your book.

2. WHAT NOT TO DO

Just like there are activities that can bring positive results, there are those that can alienate the readers, destroy potentially valuable connections, and get you blocked, fined or reported.

Do not do anything a respected publisher wouldn't do. Surprisingly many writers, for example, think it's OK to send unsolicited messages asking people they don't know personally to read their writing, swap reviews, or follow them back.

That is certainly not what a traditional publisher would do. Engaging in such activities can lead to resentment and poor reputation. It also interferes with other people's time, which is where the Rule #1 comes in.

Rule #1 - avoid wasting anyone's time

Strive to make things as nice as possible. Everything, from subscribing to a newsletter to buying a book should be simple, smooth, fast, and easy. If possible, use embedded subscription forms that make it possible for the users to subscribe on the spot just by entering their email.

When you showcase the books on your website, make sure the price, a short description, and links to the stores are easily accessible. Few things are more frustrating than poor user experience that makes one click and spend more time than necessary on buying, subscribing, or just finding the basic information.

The NOT-to-do list

Just like there is the to-do list, there is also a list of not-to-do activities. Many items on this list are against the rules of platforms such as Amazon, and some are also against the law in most of the developed countries:

1. **Sending newsletters** to anyone who hasn't knowingly and willingly subscribed.
2. **Abusing emails or contact forms** to send unsolicited messages offering your products or services.
3. **Sending messages over social media** doing the same or asking people to follow you.
4. **Promoting your books in Facebook groups or other online groups** that were not created for the purpose.
5. **Tagging people who have nothing to do with you or your post** to make them click the link.
6. **Plagiarizing, copying or stealing** anybody else's writing, design, or ideas, including ad copy, books blurbs, and book cover design.
7. **Deliberately placing your book in the wrong category** to make it seem that it ranks higher.
8. **Swap reviews or pay for reviews (this includes non-monetary incentives)** – Amazon's rules strictly forbid this, and Amazon might delete such reviews [2].
9. **Not following other rules of the platform**.

While you might be able to get away with this while flying under the radar, many of the writers who were making big money on Amazon have lost their royalties and were permanently banned from publishing on Amazon due to breaking the rules [3].

Leaving aside the ethical and moral concerns that should play a role in how you run your self-publishing business, permanently losing access to Amazon, the largest book platform in the world, is hardly worth the risk.

What's more, no traditional publisher will take a chance on a writer whose works cannot be sold on Amazon. Do this and your writing career might just be sealed.

3. MINDSET

Your mindset needs to be taken care of before you start with book promotion. I'm putting an emphasis on this because quite a few writers have a problem with promoting their work and that can block them.

There are many possible reasons why you might not be comfortable with the promotional part of self-publishing. You could, for instance, have an issue with the idea of 'selling' yourself. You might also be afraid that you'll make mistakes because you are not an expert or wish that somebody else would do this instead of you.

Identify these and then deal with them one by one. If the idea of 'selling yourself' is the problem, take an objective look at what you have written. Is the book any good, is it helpful, do you think the readers will enjoy it? If so, then you are not 'selling' yourself, you are doing something good for your readers.

Also, while it's true that you might not be an expert, remind yourself that no one else was born as one either. Once you master the ins and outs of the trade, it will become much easier. In time, you will become proficient and might even start enjoying it!

By no means is promotion a waste of time. But it might well be that you'd much rather spend your time writing than promoting. If you can afford to hire somebody else to do it, great, but know that this too can be risky since it might increase the cost but not necessarily lead to results.

One of the major benefits of learning how to do it yourself is that once you are ready and can afford to outsource the work, you will know exactly what it takes, how much it costs, and what can be achieved. You'll thus be in a much better position to negotiate and lead your self-publishing team.

Also, know that success depends on many things, ranging from the budget, quality, and appeal of your book to promotion and persistence. You are trying to make it in one of the most competitive fields.

It will not be easy, and you need to be mentally prepared for that too. It's much better to keep taking small steps regularly and opt for a slower growth rather than try to do everything at once only to end up dealing with financial and emotional burnout.

4. THE THREE BASIC QUESTIONS

When you submit your book to an agent or traditional publisher, you are bound to encounter these three questions:

- **Who is your audience?** (Who would buy this?)
- **What kind of platform do you have?** (How many, where, and who are your followers?)
- **How are you going to promote your book?** (What's your promotion strategy?)

If you cannot provide satisfactory answers to these questions, it is unlikely any traditional publisher will be interested in publishing your book.

Also, thinking you can avoid dealing with this by self-publishing is rather naive. If you want to sell, you will have to market and promote. By answering these questions, you are setting the foundations for a good book promotion campaign.

It's impossible to create a successful campaign without knowing exactly who might be interested in your book (audience), who are your followers (platform), and what would be the best way of presenting your book to them (strategy).

Some profit-oriented writers go even further and write only what they assume people would buy. They research the market, find a profitable niche, study the bestsellers in it, and then write what they think these readers would buy.

5. AUDIENCE

Start by clearly defining your audience. This is vital for every stage of your promotion since you cannot sell if you don't know who and why someone might want to read your book. Everything you do will have to send a message to that specific person.

Narrow it down

The better defined the audience, the easier it will be to come up with the promotion that will speak to the right readers. In the case of this book, for instance, my audience are self-published writers. But this doesn't mean *ALL* self-published writers since those who know how to promote obviously don't need it any longer.

My audience was thus narrowed down from *ALL* self-published writers to *THOSE* who are confused by all the options and don't know how to tackle the promotion. To narrow it down even more, the book was written for those who are self-publishing on a budget and are looking for cost-efficient and affordable options.

That's how you define the readers of your book. That makes it easier to understand their needs, why would they want to buy the book, and how to address them. Defining your readers, however, doesn't mean that nobody else but the readers in this group will buy your book.

It only means narrowing the audience down to a group that is most likely to buy your book. Promoting to this group will lead to more sales and increase the cost-efficiency of your campaign.

Audience by genre

It's much easier to define the audience for some genres than others. Advice and how-to books as well as the books in the most popular genres, for instance, are usually not a problem. Books that are further from the norm, however, can be a challenge.

That's why traditional publishers aren't keen on publishing books that cannot be easily defined and neatly placed in categories. But new authors might not even be sure in which genre to place their book. 'The Genre Guide' [4] by The Written Word Media will help you solve this problem.

If you cannot find the right genre for your book easily, you will soon find out why traditional publishers avoid publishing such books. Unless you already have a following, it will be hard to find and target the right audience. The promotion will cost more, and the results will be uncertain.

6. PLATFORM

Once you have your audience defined, it's time to build, grow, and/or expand your platform. Having a platform is of utmost importance because it allows you to reach your readers directly without having to invest in advertising.

That's also the main reason why traditional publishers and agents place so much emphasis on it. The readers who follow you and subscribe to your newsletter are the ones who will most likely be interested in your books too.

You can build your platform by blogging, guest blogging, publishing your stories in popular publications, being active on social media, and, above all, by growing your email list. Regularly posting and taking care of all this takes time and can be tedious but is a must. We'll take a closer look at these options in the following chapters.

7. BLOGGING

While you can have a blog on your author website and that's highly recommended, it will hardly bring you the visibility you need if you don't have a following. The faster route to exposure would be to start a blog on a platform where a large community already exists.

The lines between blogging and social media platforms are getting increasingly blurred. Many platforms are a mixture of both and more and more people even use their Instagram accounts as a blog. Which platform you choose thus doesn't matter as much as how well you use it.

Your choice of the platform will depend on your target audience as well. If you, for instance, write non-fiction and how-to posts, two options that might be worth considering are Medium and Quora. But there are quite a few other options too, such as Ello, Tumblr, and WordPress.

Be careful with the new blockchain or open source platforms, though. The first thing you should check for is whether the platform has a dedicated customer service. If there is just the community forum, it would be best to avoid that since there will be times when you will have to report an issue or ask for help. Open source platforms that don't have a customer service are also more prone to trolling and cyber attacks.

Another thing to consider is user interface. Some blogging platform, such as Ello and Medium have a much simpler and nicer interface than others. You can literally start writing and publishing there in minutes. Others, like

WordPress, can be a lot more complicated and thus not the best choice for a beginner.

Regardless of the platform, you'll need to invest quite a bit of effort into building a following. Do not expect to become hugely successful overnight. That's why it's also best to start with the free, simplest but nevertheless efficient option rather than the one that costs money and time to set it up.

Your choice of the platform should also depend on the community and other writers there. Is the community friendly and helpful? Do the users treat each other with respect and write the kind of posts you wouldn't be ashamed of being associated with?

It might be a good idea to test different platforms. See where you get the best results, which community makes you feel most at home, and which interface is best suited to your needs. You can also keep posting different types of posts on different platforms.

Posting interesting content regularly, commenting on other writer's stories, choosing relevant tags or categories, following other people and liking their posts, in short, being engaged and not just self-centered is how you can do well in any blogging community.

Medium

Medium might be a good place to start. It's relatively simple and easy to use but has at the same time a complex structure that offers numerous possibilities for growth. You can use it for free but there is also a $5 monthly membership option for readers who'd like to get access to member-only posts.

The membership option has no effect on your ability to use and publish on the platform for free, it only gives you the chance to earn some money if you lock your posts and write only for Medium members. Don't get too excited about the payment, though.

According to Medium's reports, more than 90% of writers who publish member-only stories earn less than $100 per month. If you opt for paid posts, you also won't be allowed to promote anything or grow your email list of subscribers. For that reason, I suggest you forget the paid option and focus on growing your email list instead.

One of the best parts of Medium is clean and simple interface. All you need to do to start writing is open an account, click on your profile pic, select 'New story,' and type. Medium automatically saves the draft as you type, so you won't even have to worry about that.

It's not as hard to get followers on Medium as it can be on some other platforms. The community is nice and there is a responsive customer service. You can publish most anything on Medium, from fiction to advice and essays. Fiction is not as popular, though, and writers who publish how-to posts and commentaries tend to fare better.

Medium's editors select featured stories, and these are promoted more. It seems that the editors give preference to journalism and not as much to other forms of writing. Visit Medium's homepage to see what kind of posts and topics have been featured by the staff to get an idea of what the editors prefer.

As more and more writers flock to Medium, the views of most stories seem to be decreasing. Nevertheless, Medium remains a good place for a beginner to hone his or her writing skills, gain the following, and test the readers' response.

Another unique feature on Medium is the option to create publications. Having a publication lets you publish stories by other writers in addition to your own. You can also publish your stories in numerous other publications on Medium and that can give your posts additional exposure.

There are hundreds of publications on Medium. They vary in the kind of stories they publish and topics they cover. Some of them have many thousands of followers and other only a handful. Trying to get published in the more popular ones can be a challenge and it's much easier to get your work into the ones with fewer followers.

Medium doesn't offer any insight into the ranking of the publications, so it's hard to know which one to choose. But there is an app created by a member of the community that solves this problem. Top Pub [5] ranks most of the publications on Medium by the number of followers and shows what topics these publications cover.

Another interesting but rather annoying feature on Medium is that it treats comments like blog posts. This turns into a problem when you connect RSS feed of your blog to your Amazon or Goodreads author page, for it shows your comments as if they were blog posts.

Ello

Ello was created by artists for artists. You will find writers, photographers, illustrators, designers, and other creators there. This can be helpful if you are looking for an illustrator or designer. One of the best things about Ello is that it's meant to be a place where you can showcase your work. It's very easy to sell books and other products on Ello.

When creating a new post, simply upload the product's picture, click 'Sell,' and link to the store (for a book, for instance, to Amazon). Ello is also focused on connecting agencies, publishers, and creators. You can add 'Hire' or 'Collaborate' buttons to your profile if you are available for work.

Like Medium, Ello has a clean layout and user-friendly interface. It is a free, simple, and easy blogging/social platforms solution you can set up in minutes. You'll find one of the nicest online communities for creators there.

One of the major drawbacks at the time of writing this, however, is that the posts do not look good when you share them on social media. For some reason, the sub-headline gets all messed up. Another downside is that there is no subscription form option.

Quora

Quora can be used as a blogging platform but is above all a place where people post questions – either for practical reasons or due to curiosity. You can get a lot of exposure if you write a good response to a question. Several writers reported that regularly publishing on Quora increased their following and traffic to their website.

Quora also sends a daily email newsletter with a selection of most interesting questions, which is a goldmine for content ideas. You will find out what people are curious about and what kind of issues they need help dealing with. You will also come across some of the most surprising stories that make life weirder than fiction.

Quora is not that great as a traditional blogging platform, though, and there is no subscription form option that would let you build your email list either. You can, however, get traction and drive visits to your blog or website. As such, it can be a useful tool.

Tumblr

Tumblr is another interesting platform with many useful features, such as the option to connect your domain. Community on Tumblr, however, is a bit specific. It can be hard to get followers or any reactions to the posts.

Many artists and illustrators use Tumblr since visually strong posts, mood boards, and images tend to do better and gain the following faster. Also, things to do with the unusual, occult, and witchcraft might do well on Tumblr.

Like on WordPress, you can pick a theme for your blog on Tumblr. Many of these, however, are not free and are sold by external developers. This means that solving any issues you might run into using these themes will depend on the developer.

Tumblr could be an interesting option because it lets you connect a domain and is thus also a hosting service. This means that it can serve as your personal website, which might be a nice and affordable solution, especially if you don't have a website yet.

Another great feature is that it allows you to reblog other users' posts as well as content from the web. Tumblr displays these posts nicely on your blog's homepage. You can thus use it to curate interesting content from all over the web.

Tumblr, however, is also more complicated and less intuitive than Medium and Ello. Also, Tumblr's future is a bit uncertain since it's been recently acquired by Verizon's Oath. On the other hand, though, this could be a good thing since the platform might get a chance for renewal.

WordPress

WordPress is the most complicated platform of them all. To begin with, there is WordPress.com and then there is WordPress.org. WordPress.org is an open source platform that lets you build complex websites. It, however, takes quite a bit of learning.

With WordPress.org, you'll also need to take care of your own hosting and acquire plugins for full functionality and safety. Many of these addons aren't free and have to be regularly updated.

What's more, the free themes are not that great, and you will likely have to invest in a nicer theme too. Like on Tumblr, themes are sold by external developers and you have to be careful with that.

WordPress.com, on the other hand, is more like a website builder and thus easier to use. But the free plan doesn't allow you to connect your domain and, as a bigger problem, it displays ads on your blog from which you'll earn nothing. You will thus have to opt for a paid plan just to get rid of the ads.

Patreon

While you cannot exactly use Patreon as a blogging platform, you can use it to find supporters (patrons) and connect with them through patron-only posts. This is an alternative to member-only or locked content option you can have on your website.

Patreon is growing in popularity since many artists and writers find it hard to survive. With Patreon, even writers who don't publish in highly commercial genres stand a chance of getting at least some monthly support with the help of their patrons.

Patreon makes a member-only option for paid content easy to set up and that is especially useful if you don't have a website. Also, Patreon is a community and you can share both free and locked posts there. This can give your posts greater exposure.

On the other hand, though, it's hard to find supporters who'd be willing to invest in your work with monthly donations. Patreon might thus not be great for a beginner but could be useful after you already have a following.

8. GUEST BLOGGING

Guest blogging is a great way of reaching a wider audience – especially if you write advice or how-to posts and manage to get your writing in highly popular blogs. Many blogs have submission guidelines for guest bloggers but even if the guidelines are nowhere to be found, you can ask whether they'd be interested in your contributions.

Sometimes you can get paid for guest blogging, but what you usually receive is a byline – a picture and one or two sentences about you at the end of the post. Use this to promote your work and include the link to your website, books, or blog.

A byline may not sound like much, but it's valuable. It not only leads to clicks but also serves as a backlink to your website. This is important for SEO reasons since it increases Google's ranking of your website.

You can also use your guest blog posts as a reference. The more popular the site, the more valuable that is. To get published on popular blogs, though, you'l have to pitch an idea and already have something to show. Typically, that would be the link to your website, social media accounts, and your top performing blog posts.

Here is an example of a successful pitch I sent to Mark Dawson's Self-Publishing Formula blcg [6]:

Blog topic: Why you don't really need author website when starting out (you do need an online presence, though)

Premise: There is this ill-conceived notion that one needs an author website when starting out - that's not necessarily true. What one needs is a strong online presence, but that can be achieved in many ways, such as blogging, author page on Books2Read and Goodreads, social media, and, yes, at a certain point an author website too. Websites can be expensive (in more than one way) and not worth the investment until one has some following.

I self-published two books and am working on two more. I've built my following and pushed my book to #1 in three categories on Amazon without a website. I now have a website (matejaklaric.com), but I'm still not quite happy with it. Bottom line - a lot can be done without it and it's hard to build a good one too.

I'd be happy to share what I learned with your readers.

Cheers,

Mateja

In most cases, you will be expected to submit original work written especially for the blog and will not be allowed to republish the post anywhere else, not even your website. Many blogs will also expect you to refrain from publishing a similar post elsewhere for at least a couple of months after they first published it.

To be on the safe side, ask about the policy on this if you plan on doing anything of the sort. The last thing you need is getting banned from writing for a popular blog.

9. PUBLICATIONS

Publishing your work in publications is another option that can give your stories additional exposure. Unless you are writing non-fiction and would like to be paid for the post, you also won't be expected to pitch.

Especially when it comes to fiction, the editors are above all interested in the quality of your story rather than qualifications and credentials. Most publications will let you have a byline at the end of the story where you can link to the website or books you wish to promote.

A word of warning, though – avoid publications that charge writers reading fees. Your goal is not to pay to be published but rather get paid for the published work. Besides, the online world is full of places where you can publish for free.

That's one of the reasons why I recommend Medium for blogging. You can easily submit your stories to many publications on the same platform where you blog. You can even publish a story first on your profile and then submit it to a publication too.

A few publications might only accept unpublished drafts, but most won't mind if you already published it. You cannot, however, have your story published in more than one publication on Medium and most publications also won't be happy if you later remove the story and publish it in another publication.

The previously mentioned Top Pub application [5] will help you find the right Medium publications for the type of your posts. You will also see how many followers the publication has and what kind of exposure you can expect from publishing there.

10. SOCIAL MEDIA

We all have a problem with limited hours in a day, and that's why many writers hate dealing with social media or prefer to only focus on one or two accounts. You don't have to do everything at once, though.

You might not end up being active on all social media accounts, but you should at least understand the options they give you. There are major differences between them and you need to choose the best ones for your books.

While some best-selling authors might not have a social media presence, most of them do [7]. But being active on social media is not just about building a following and selling your books. It's also about connecting with your readers and writing community.

Make sure to use appropriate and relevant hashtags when sharing your posts. Many blogging platforms use tags or categories instead of hashtags, but they all serve the same purpose – they help the readers find the posts on topics they are interested in.

Include the link to your website, blog, or books in your social media profiles too. Make it easy for people to learn more about your work. Also, pin the post about your latest success, special offer, or a new book to the top of your profile.

If you don't have a website or would like to share more than one link in your social media profiles, use Linktree [8]. Linktree is an online app that creates a menu with different links so that you can share them under a single URL.

Facebook

Despite growing competition, Facebook remains the undisputed king of social media and most people at least occasionally use it. It's also a popular social media option among successful self-published writers.

The main reasons for this are its features, such as groups, paid ads, and shops. Facebook recently formed a partnership with Instagram and that turned the two into a force to be reckoned with.

Business page

You'll have to create a Facebook business page to run ad campaigns, boost posts, sell products, and connect your Instagram account so that you can run ads there too. You won't have access to these options through your personal account, but it's best to remain active on both, for what you post on your private profile will be seen by more people than what you post on your business profile.

The reason for this is that Facebook wants you to pay for the boost of the post on your business account and limits their visibility if you don't. The best way around this is to be active on your personal profile or create a group to connect with your readers and only use a business account to set up paid promotions and create a shop.

Groups

Groups are one of the best parts of Facebook. You can, for instance, create a group for your fans and connect it to your business page. It's a good idea to join some groups for writers too. There are several helpful communities where you can get feedback and useful information.

Things change fast in the world of self-publishing, and you are most likely to hear about the latest news in one of the Facebook groups first. But follow the rules – each group has its own rules and was created for a different purpose. You risk getting thrown out if you spam.

Instagram

If you think Instagram is only for those who publish pretty pictures and photos, you are mistaken. The profiles of those who work in the marketing and publishing industry either as writers or promotors are growing in popularity. Some even use Instagram as an additional blogging platform and post short stories next to the pics.

You can no longer ignore Instagram, and even less so since its partnership with Facebook opened new possibilities for promotion. To see how successful authors use Instagram check Jay Kristoff's (@misterkristoff) [9] and Victoria Schwab's (@veschwab) [10] profiles.

Business account

You can turn your personal Instagram account into a business account and get access to advertising and additional features, such as analytics that gives you insight into your audience (age, gender, location…).

Instagram offers free training to help you set up and use these options [11]. You can also sell products with shoppable posts [12]. This option, however, is only available in selected countries, and in addition to having an Instagram business account, you'll also have to set up the shop on your Facebook business page first.

Twitter

Many bloggers, writers, and readers use Twitter. Having a Twitter account is especially recommended if you blog on Medium. Ev Williams, the founder of Medium, was also one of the founders of Twitter and the two platforms are closely connected.

Medium's editors, readers, and writers are active on Twitter and you might find it easier to grow following if you blog on Medium. Many book reviewers, authors, and publishers also use Twitter.

You can also advertise on Twitter, but that has lately become ridiculously expensive. You can end up paying $5 for a click or two, which is more expensive than Facebook or Instagram [13].

LinkedIn

LinkedIn was created for a very specific audience – working professional and businesses. If you publish non-fiction related to business, LinkedIn is the place to be. You can also advertise this kind of books there.

Google+

Google+ is lagging behind most other social media. I nevertheless included it because I could see from my stats that my blog posts get views from Google+ too. The profile doesn't take much maintenance and if it brings in additional views, it doesn't hurt to keep it.

You can also create collections on Google+, which is an interesting feature that can attract more followers. Collections are used for topic-related content. I have, for instance, a collection for the posts from my publication *The Rabbit Is In*.

Pinterest

Pictures are what Pinterest is mostly about, but you can share the links to blog posts or books too. One of the great features of Pinterest is that your pins remain visible and don't disappear into oblivion as soon as you publish them. Like Gogle+, running a Pinterest account doesn't take much effort and can bring you additional views.

Pinterest is trying to keep up with the most popular social media and has lately started to experiment with business accounts as well. The advantage of converting your personal account to business profile is that you might be able to sell products, promote pins, and get access to analytics.

Pin promotion, however, is only available to users in selected countries, but access to analytics is open to everyone. It will give you an insight into which of your pins are doing well and what kind of content generates most clicks.

Reddit

In 2018, social platform Reddit surpassed Facebook and became the third most-visited site on the web [14]. This alone is a good enough reason to open an account there and see what it's all about.

Reddit is basically a place where people share links to interesting posts and engage in discussions. It's composed of various subcommunities called subreddits. Each of these subreddits is run by a different team and has thus different guidelines and rules.

There are numerous subreddits for writers on Reddit. In some, you can publish your stories and showcase your writing. Two examples are r/nosleep for horror stories [15] and r/shortstories [16] for short stories.

In 2018, Reddit also started to experiment with advertising. Due to the controversial nature of the platform that is, unfortunately, also known for subreddits where misogyny, hate speech, trolling, and pornography roamed freely, advertisers remain cautious [17].

11. E-MAIL LIST OF SUBSCRIBERS

As already stated, the main benefit of an email list is the ability to reach the readers directly, without having to pay a cent for ads and promotion. Your e-mail list of subscribers is thus a crucial part of your platform and even more important than the following on social media accounts.

If you build your email list correctly, your subscribers will be truly interested in your work and that's what you need. If you, however, start building your email list by offering baits, the subscribers probably won't be as interested in your content as they were in getting something for free.

How to get subscribers

The best way of building a high-quality e-mail list is to have the subscription form on your blog, website, and in ebooks. Above all, you want emails from the readers who like your writing and would like to see more of it.

Another popular way of doing this is by asking for emails in exchange for a free offer, gift, or participation in a giveaway contest. If you offer an incentive (bait) that has little or nothing to do with your writing, however, this will not lead to a high-quality email list.

Quality over quantity

Having a small high-quality email list is better than having many subscribers who only subscribed because they wanted to win a prize. These might never open any of your newsletters, let alone show interest in your books.

What's more, e-mail subscription services, such as MailChimp, charge their fees based on the size of your email list. Maintaining a large list of disinterested subscribers will thus also cost more but not lead to the desired results.

The measure of quality

You can measure the quality of your list by the percentage of subscribers who open your newsletter as well as the percentage of those who then also click on the links. MailChimp – the email marketing service I recommend – shows you the average open and click rates in the industry so that you can compare those with yours.

The current average open rate in the publishing and media industry in MailChimp, for instance, is 15.09%. Everything about that is good – the higher, the better. The average open rate of my list, for example, is around 36%. My list is not huge, but I have subscribers who are interested in my work, and that's what matters more than the list's size.

Conversion rates

How many subscribers can you expect to get from offering one of your ebooks for free in exchange for an email? Unless your work is already popular and in high demand, low conversion rates are common.

According to Sumo, for instance, less than 2% is the average conversion rate [18]. This means that out of every 100 people who see a subscription form, 1 or 2 might subscribe. This percentage, of course, can be lower or higher, and it, among other things, depends on the type, incentive, and placement of the form.

Subscription forms

There are three main types of subscription forms: embedded forms, online subscription forms you can link to, and pop-up forms. The most efficient are embedded and pop-up forms. Pop-up forms can be tricky, though, so use them with caution.

The main thing that increases the conversion rate is whether the readers can subscribe by simply entering the email without being taken to an external site. Another equally important factor is when and where is the form displayed.

Embedded forms

Many website builders and some blogging platforms have an embedded subscription form. This can be either a part of the platform or an external app, plugin, or HTML code.

On Medium, for instance, embedded forms are not an inbuilt part of the platform, but you can use Upscribe [19], an email subscription service developed for Medium users. Simply paste the Upscribe's link in the draft of your story and hit return. This will automatically turn the link into an embedded form.

This can be a bit of a drag since you'll have to do it manually every single time you write a new post. Upscribe has recently also started to charge monthly subscription fees that are rather steep. On the other hand, though, their forms tend to convert well.

If you use WordPress, you'll need a plugin to create an embedded form. Most of these options are free, but there are many you can choose from [20]. You'll thus have to sieve through them to find the one with least glitches and best suited to your needs.

On Tumblr, you'll have to use a theme that includes an embedded form feature (not all of them do) or use an HTML code.

Online subscription forms

Even though not the best option, linking to an online subscription form (landing page) is sometimes the only option. In ebooks, for instance, you'll have to use the link to such form. To create it, sign up for one of the many email marketing services, such as MailChimp.

MailChimp is a good choice for a writer on a budget since it offers a free plan for up to 2,000 subscribers. On the downside, though, it doesn't have the most user-friendly interface and it will take some time before you get used to it.

As another option, if you blog on Medium and plan on paying the Upscribe's monthly fee anyway, you can use Upscribe since the app gives you the links to a subscription landing page as well as the embedded form.

Pop-up and other fancy forms

Pop-up and other fancy subscription forms are a tempting option and can be highly efficient too. They come with more than one caveat, though, so be careful how you use them. They are a matter of much controversy since not every pop-up form is a good pop-up form [21].

The main problem with pop-ups (or poop-ups, as some 'lovingly' call them) is that it's very easy to annoy and lose your website visitors because of them. The recommended use of pop-up forms is to show them only when visitors are about to exit your site. Do not bug people while they are browsing or reading the content on your website.

Another option is a banner placed at the bottom or top of the page. To use these forms, you'll need to use a service such as AddThis [22] and insert HTML code in your blogging platform or website. Not every platform makes this possible, or at least not on every plan. Such codes can sometimes also interfere with the code on your website.

What to include in the form

Remember the Rule #1? Do NOT waste anyone's time. This means that you should only ask your subscribers for what you need, and what you need in this case is their email. You don't need to know their name or have any other personal information, so don't ask for that.

In addition to a call to action (e.g. Sign up!), also briefly state why it's a good idea to subscribe and what can they expect from that. This means letting them know how often you are going to send newsletters and what kind of content can they expect.

Making this clear will also take care of the GDPR, based on which you are obligated to let your subscribers know which part of their personal information (in this case their email) and for what purpose (e.g. sending newsletters and how often) you are going to use.

Sending newsletters

Sending newsletters is an art that involves the right kind of content, frequency, and newsletter design as well as a reliable delivery service. In general, the content should be informative and engaging rather than salesy, the emails sent sparingly, and the design as simple as possible.

There are many email marketing services, but not all of them are affordable and reliable. You want to be sure that your emails reach the mailboxes of your subscribers and don't end up in their spam folders instead and that's another important reason why I recommend MailChimp.

MailChimp is one of the oldest and most reliable services. It can be integrated with most any other platform, from major website builders to apps. This alone will save you time, for the new emails will be automatically synced with your MailChimp list and you won't have to import them manually every time someone subscribes.

Common newsletter mistakes

It's hard to get subscribers but easy to lose them. Avoid making mistakes that could cause your readers to unsubscribe.

Unless you sell online courses and already have a community that is deeply interested in your teaching and guidance, avoid sending daily email campaigns. Also, keep in mind that people subscribed to get interesting content and not sales pitches about your books.

You can mention these, but do not make the email mainly about what you have to sell. Newsletter, as the name suggests, should be about news. Also, as a writer, you tell stories. You can even tell the news as a story.

Include personal information about your writing process – things that cannot be found anywhere else, but avoid doing the following:

- **Sending too many emails.** No one enjoys being bombarded with messages and nothing is easier than unsubscribing. If your subscribers start to unsubscribe, too many emails might be the reason.

- **Making your email look like a shop.** What your readers want to see is your writing. Unless you have a new book coming out and would like to show them the book cover or illustrations, leave the product pictures out and focus on the message.

- **Writing too long newsletters.** If you have, for some reason, a lot to say, break down the message into sections and divide them with subheadings. This would make it easier for your readers to skip the parts they might not be interested in.

- **Going overboard with design.** Keeping it simple is the best policy. You are a writer. Simple white background and easy-to-read font, and perhaps a small logo or a profile pic are more than enough.

- **Not understanding why people subscribed and what they expect from the newsletter.** What the subscribers most likely want are your stories, interesting updates, and staying in the know.

Automated emails

Automated emails are another one of those options that can be tricky and off-putting. It's very hard to create automated emails in a way that doesn't make it clear that they've been automated.

That's why I wouldn't recommend them to a beginner or at least wouldn't place them at the top of your priority list. It's much more efficient to stay personal and simply let them know when you publish new stories and blog posts, inform them about writing projects you are working on, and send them other relevant information and news.

There is, however, one automated option that might be useful. In MailChimp, you can send an automated email to every new subscriber. If you, for example, ran a campaign where you offered a gift (e.g. your ebook) as an incentive, you can use the automated email response to send new subscribers the link to where they can download their gift.

I recommend using Dropbox [23] for the downloads since it will let you can set up the date when the link expires. You can thus avoid the link being used after the campaign ended, so that the ebook won't stay permanently available to anyone who'd get access to the link.

12. NETWORKING & GROUPS

Never underestimate the power of networking. Growing a network of connections is a great investment of your time and effort. Use your website, blog, and social media to connect with your readers, but also connect with other writers and members of writing communities.

Writers' groups & communities

I've got my first podcast interview as a writer in one of the Facebook groups. One of the writers there asked whether anyone would be interested in being a guest on her podcast and I jumped at the opportunity. An interview is free promotion so be alert and don't miss out on such chances.

Another benefit of being an active member in online groups and writing communities is access to the latest self-publishing news, tips, and insider information you'll get from other writers. In many of them, you'll also be able to ask for feedback on your book cover or blurb.

There are many groups for writers on Facebook and Goodreads. Make sure to check the communities' rules first, though. Self-promotion, for instance, is banned or limited to specific threads in most groups.

You can also create your own Facebook group and connect it to your Facebook business page. Use it as a place where you connect with your fans and assemble the so-called street team.

Street teams

Street team is what writer's most devoted fans and supporters are called when they help with book launches. Many writers create Facebook groups to organize activities related to the launch, such as a promotion of a preorder, giveaways, and free offers. Street team members help you share and spread the news about these activities. They are usually the first to post reviews as well.

13. FREE AUTHOR PAGES

Creating free author pages on book-related platforms is highly recommended. At the very least, make sure you set up your author page on Amazon Author Central since it's connected to the Amazon product pages of your books.

Many book promotion sites, such as BookBub, also offer free author pages. Recommended platforms are also Goodreads and Books2Read. You can use Books2Read's author's page as your landing page if you don't yet have a website.

Amazon Author Central

Creating your author page on Amazon Author Central is of crucial importance because it is connected to your book's product page on Amazon. You can edit and add important parts to your book description, such as editorial reviews, in Author Central.

Editorial reviews are the only kind of reviews Amazon allows you to pay for, but you should never include them or ask anyone to paste them in the customer review section. If you decide to use paid reviews, only use them in the Editorial Reviews section. Alternatively, you can also post praise you received from your readers or fellow writers in this section.

You can also add events, photos, and videos to your Amazon Author Central page. If you have a book video trailer, for instance, upload it here. Importantly, don't forget to connect your blog's RSS feed as well.

Adding RSS feed

The RSS feed option on Amazon Author Central and in Goodreads lets you connect your blog to your author pages. Excerpts and links to your blog posts will thus be displayed there and drive traffic to your blog.

To find your blog's RSS link, click the RSS icon on your website and copy the link. If you don't have a website, your RSS feed link will depend on the platform. For RSS feed on Medium, for instance, insert '/feed/' between the Medium domain and your username.

On Tumblr, as another example, you'll have to add /rss at the end of your blog's URL. The directions can usually be found in the help section of the platforms or you can contact support if you have trouble finding it.

Goodreads

Goodreads is a community of millions of book lovers and authors. It was acquired by Amazon in 2013 [24] and the two platforms are now closely connected. If you use Amazon's Kindle for reading, for example, you can add the ebook you are reading to your Goodreads page.

Goodreads also lets you add apps and widgets to your website. You can, for instance, create a button that lets the visitors on your website add your books to their Goodreads page with one click. Another app displays your book's Goodreads rating.

The platform, however, doesn't have the most user-friendly interface and can be difficult to navigate. Also, it has some weird rule. Goodreads, for instance, won't let you change the book cover once you've uploaded it.

Even though you will thus be able to change the cover on Amazon (which is not uncommon, since writers often test different versions of the covers), Goodreads won't let you change it. Keep that in mind and perhaps only upload the cover when you're sure you will keep it.

Books2Read author page

If you don't have a website yet, creating a free author page on Books2Read and using that as your landing page can be a great temporary solution. If you already have a domain (which is highly recommended), simply redirect it to your Books2Read author page.

I recommend Books2Read because you can set up your author page up in minutes, it has a nice design and is focused on your books. It also includes the links to social media accounts and you can use 'Follow me' button to grow your email list by linking the button to your online subscription form.

The page also includes a place for a short bio and thus covers all the basics. To make this clear, though, I do not recommend going without a website indefinitely, but using Books2Read's author page is a perfect and above all free solution for a writer on a budget who doesn't have the time and money for a website yet.

I built the following of my blog on Medium to close to 5,000, started to grow my email list, and managed to get my second book to #1 in more than one category on Amazon without having a website. I used my author page on

Books2Read as my landing page instead and that worked well enough for a start [25].

Books2Read is a sister website to Draft2Digital. If you already have an account on Draft2Digital and publish your books there, you will be able to log in using the same account and your books will be automatically included in your Books2Read author page. You don't have to publish on Draft2Digital, though, to be able to create your author page on Books2Read.

14. WEBSITE, DOMAIN & EMAIL

Building a website takes time and money but will not bring any major results if you have no followers. For a beginner, a website is thus not a top priority while having a blog and/or social media presence, building a following, and growing an email list is.

That's not to say that it's not recommended to launch a proper author website at some point, and I'm certainly not arguing against that. But what you need to do as a matter of top priority is buy a domain and redirect it to your blog or landing page rather than build a website.

Don't trust those who claim that you can have your website up and running in a matter of hours. If you have never tried to build a website, have no clue what hosting and cPanel are, or which website builder and theme to choose, it will take a whole lot more than a couple of hours and it certainly won't be that easy.

This chapter will help you understand what it takes to build and run a website. It will also show you how to avoid costly and nerve-racking mistakes. These can range from having your site hacked (open-source platforms can be risky) to having a website marked as not-safe by Google (no SSL certificate).

That's one of the main reasons why I recommend taking it slow with a website and temporarily use an author page that is safely hosted by a reliable platform instead. Besides, you want your website to last and not waste your time on having to build a new one next year. Take the time to explore the options before making any decision you might regret later.

One of the major benefits of running a blog on an established platform, such as Medium or Tumblr, is that the platform takes care of any potential safety issues and hosting. You are thus free from worries and can focus solely on writing and publishing. On the other hand, though, you could do a lot more with your website.

But then again, the numbers of hours in a day are limited and so is your budget. You need to make the most of what little budget you can afford to invest. That's why we are looking for cost-efficient and affordable options rather than on what we wish we would if we only could.

One of the options, for instance, is running a blog on Tumblr, connecting or redirecting your domain to it, and using that as your website. An example of how one can run a business with nothing but a blog and social media account is *Lisa's Lost in Lit* on Tumblr and the related Instagram account *lifeinlit* with over 75K followers [26]. Lisa didn't even bother to connect a domain!

While you, as a writer, can follow Lisa's suit when it comes to building a following with blogging and social media, you do need a domain. The domain should ideally be the name you use as an author, whether that's your real or pen name.

Domain

Imagine being the next J.K. Rowling and not having bought the domain with your name (jkrowling.com). For Rowling, that could have been a costly mistake. She either didn't make it or had to pay a whole lot of money to buy it off if anyone managed to beat her to it.

As an author, your name is your brand. That's why securing your name as a domain is a matter of top priority. In marketing, a brand is everything. If you are serious about your writing, you need to invest in that even if you don't plan on creating a website just yet.

Where NOT to buy a domain

Don't buy a domain on a website builder, such as Weebly, Wix, Squarespace or any other builder, even if they offer it for free. You need full control over your domain and if you buy it there, you are giving that control away. Doing this can make it harder and costly to move your website to another platform later.

The recommended way of doing this is thus by buying the domain and hosting plan on one of the independent hosting services. This will let you easily switch between website platforms, redirect or point your domain, and have full control over your emails.

Hosting services and emails

Hosting services operate like a relay station where you can choose where to point or redirect your domain as well as create email addresses using the domain name (e.g. YourName@YourDomain.com).

When you, for instance, point (connect) your domain to a website builder where you have created your website, your website will become accessible on your domain URL. If you, on the other hand, redirect your domain instead of pointing it, the visitors will be redirected to another site when accessing your domain.

If you decide to connect your domain to your blog on Tumblr, for instance, you will point your domain to Tumblr. If, however, you opt for an author page on Books2Read as your landing page, you will have to redirect your domain to your author page URL because Books2Read doesn't have the option of connecting a custom domain.

Hosting services also let you create various email addresses. You can get away with only having an email on Gmail these days, but it looks more professional if you use an email with your domain name.

What to look for in a hosting service

The hosting service has to be reliable, safe, and with globally distributed servers. That's necessary for fast delivery of emails, regardless of where in the world they were sent to or from. If you decide to build your website on open source platform, such as WordPress, good hosting is also important because you want your website to load fast.

Much like with blogs and other platforms, reliable 24/7 customer service is also important. This is even more so when it comes to hosting services. Good customer service will help you with everything you might need and fast. If you are new to this, you will need to talk with someone to help you figure things out.

The best option is chat. If a hosting service doesn't have a reliable 24/7 chat option, do not use it. There are two reasons for this – first, it instantly connects you to a real person, and second, everything will be written down and you can have a copy sent to you in an email. This makes poor treatment less likely.

cPanel

cPanel is a standard dashboard provided by your hosting service. This is where, among other things, you can manage and point your domains or access the emails.

Website builders

Now that you have secured your domain, it's time to start looking for website options. You can either use Tumblr or WordPress as blogging platforms that can also serve as websites, or use website builders, such as Squarespace, Weebly or Strikingly. This is the list of features you should pay attention to:

- high-quality customer service
- https/SSL certificate for safety
- supported on all major browsers
- high-quality themes
- mobile responsive themes
- simple user interface
- features such as blog and shop
- social media following and sharing buttons
- subscription form options
- access to HTML
- stats and analytics
- integrations (e.g. MailChimp, Google Analytics)

- reasonable price and plans
- free trial period
- refund options

Make sure to test the platform first to see how easy it is to use it. Be careful with the refund terms and at least at the beginning opt for a monthly rather than yearly plan. Most website builders only offer a short trial period. Issues, however, might start showing after you are already on a paid plan and no longer eligible for a refund.

Content & design

You also need content and design for your website. You will have to create a visual identity based on the genre of your books. If you write romance, for instance, your site will look differently from a horror writer's. You will thus have to choose the right theme, colors, fonts, and images [27].

And then there is content, a section about you, your books, blogs, and links. Importantly, the content has to be SEO friendly [28] so that the site ranks higher on Google and gets more organic traffic. As you can see, building a good and functional website is not that easy and will most certainly take more than just a few hours.

15. YOUR BOOK AS A TOOL

Think of the front and back matter of your book (the pages before and after the story) as a place where you can promote your books, grow your email list, and tell the reader more about yourself.

As a writer on a budget, you need to make use of any free advertising you can get. The pages at the front and back of your books are this free advertising space. What's more, they are the space where you will find your readers for sure.

Promote your other books

If the readers liked your book, they will want to know more about you and read your other books too. You can include a list of them at the front and then again at the back. At the back, you can also add a short description to each book. In ebooks, link the books to where the readers can buy them, and promote upcoming releases as well.

Grow your email list

Create an online subscription form and invite your readers to subscribe for your newsletter. Place the invitation at the end of the ebook and link the text (e.g. Subscribe…) to your online subscription form.

You can also create a button in addition to the text. To do that, use image manipulation programs or an online app such as Snappa or Canva. Create a button with call-to-action (e.g.

Sign up), insert it as an image in your ebook, and link it to the subscription form.

Some writers recommend offering an incentive (also known as the reader's magnet), such as a free ebook or a short story in return for the reader's emails. The success of this, however, depends on the book and other factors.

I tried this approach in my book *How to Self-Publish the Fast, Free & Easy Way* and 1% of the readers subscribed to get this one for free. Conversion and click-through rates for subscription forms and ads are often below 1%, so don't expect too much.

Ask for reviews

Not everyone agrees on whether it's OK to ask you readers for a review at the end of the book. It might depend on the book, but many writers (including myself) feel there is nothing wrong with that.

Bio and links

Use front or back matter of the book to introduce yourself to the readers and tell them more about you. If you write advice and how-to books, for example, tell them about your credentials and experiences that make you the right person to write about the topic.

If you write fiction, tell them something about your life. Share what inspires you or even where you got the idea for the book. If they liked the book, they will be interested in you as its author too. Don't forget to include the links to your website or blog.

16. BOOK COVER DESIGN

One of the most crucial parts of book marketing and promotion is book cover design. This is even more important when it comes to certain genres where the readers expect to see high-quality covers and a certain style.

In general, book cover design works much like the packaging in consumer products. Companies invest a lot of money in it because they know that buyers make decisions based on visual impressions. In highly competitive fields, the packaging can literally make or break the sale.

Much like big businesses, traditional publishers tend to spend a lot of money on book covers. Berrett-Koehler Publishers, for instance, invest from $1,500 for standard to $4,000 for blockbuster book covers [29].

That, however, doesn't mean that you'll have to spend that much [30]. The investment in the book cover will depend on the genre as well as how much talent for design you have. But above all, you need to understand the role of a good cover design and what it should achieve.

The role of a good book cover design

Book cover design plays an important role in the buyer's journey for various reasons. In general, a good book cover will help the reader:

- notice the book among many others,
- instantly recognize the genre,

- get an idea of what the book is about.

Based on the cover, the reader will either take a closer look or keep browsing. Books don't exist in a vacuum. They are presented to readers in an ocean of other books and that's why they need to stand out and not just look nice on their own.

When evaluating the cover, take into consideration how and where readers find books. Usually, this happens in online stores, such as Amazon. The book covers there are displayed at the smallest size and there are hundreds upon hundreds of books too.

If you cover doesn't stand out, it will likely get overlooked just because of that. The first thing you thus need to take care of is making sure your cover draws attention to it. When evaluating the cover design, always check the following:

- the cover looks good at the smallest size,
- you can notice it among many other books,
- the title is easy to read at the smallest size.

Before you start designing your book cover, take the time to study other covers in the genre. The best way of doing this would be by not only browsing through books on Amazon but by also subscribing to traditional publishers' as well as book promotion sites' newsletters (more on book promotion sites in Chapter 28).

That's how you get in touch with the latest trends and see what others are doing. This will also give you an idea of how high (or low) is the book cover bar set in your book's category.

Non-fiction

Readers are usually less demanding when it comes to non-fiction genres, such as guides and how-to books. With these, it's easier to get away with an ugly cover as long as the readers notice it.

If the topic is of interest to the readers, they will buy the book regardless of the cover's beauty or the lack of it. The main thing here is the title – it must be easy to read and clearly inform about the content of the book.

That doesn't mean that the attractiveness of the cover doesn't play a role, of course it does. That just means that in non-fiction, a cover is usually not as crucial for sales as it is in fiction (especially in highly competitive genres).

Images also tend to be less important for non-fiction. Simple designs prevail, often only using typography or simple forms. You will thus more likely be able to create a decent book cover for non-fiction yourself. Book cover templates in Snappa or Canva are a good place to start.

Fiction

If you have no experience in design, you'll have to hire a designer or buy a premade book cover for fiction. In less competitive genres and with some effort, however, you might be able to create a cover for fiction yourself.

In some popular genres, such as fantasy and YA the readers are used to top-notch covers and easily recognizable styles. Book cover designs in these genres often call for demanding Photoshop techniques, merging several images into one, and using special effects. Certain types of fonts are also used.

You can hardly do that in Snappa or Canva, and if the cover design isn't on par with other books in the genre, this will have a negative impact on the sales. Book cover designers, however, can be expensive. High-end covers can cost hundreds or even thousands of dollars, but it's nevertheless possible to find more affordable options too.

You can, for instance, find good designers on Upwork and get a book cover for less than $100. You'll have to find someone whose style fits your needs, though, and provide them with clear directions.

If you have a problem with that and no idea what you want, try premade book cover design websites. You can find decent covers for less than $100 on websites such as The Book Cover Designer [31] and The Cover Vault [32].

Good designers and artists can also be found on ArtStation, Tumblr, Ello, and Pixabay. Using unique artwork might be worth the price for some genres if you can afford that. Artists from all over the world showcase their work on these sites, so you might be able to get a good deal.

If you are not using original artwork, make sure that the designer has the rights for all the images they used in your book cover. Neglecting that could lead to trouble due to copyright issues.

DIY cover design

If you decide to design your own book cover, prepare to spend quite a bit of time on that. You will need to either buy or find copyright free fonts and images, as well as choose and learn how to use the right program for the task.

Programs and apps

There are many different programs and online apps you can use to create book covers. Some writers use Microsoft Word or PowerPoint, others GIMP, and still others online design apps, such as Snappa or Canva.

Snappa and Canva are the easiest for a beginner. Their user-interfaces are intuitive, and you can start designing based on existing ebook cover templates. This gives you a starting point and makes the process faster and easier.

There are limits, however, to what you can do with these rather simple apps. I prefer Snappa due to free images and more options for image manipulation. The selection of fonts, however, is better on Canva.

GIMP [33] is a good option for complex designs. It's an open-source program and thus free to use. Its functionality is much like Photoshop's and you can use multiple layers. The program can be hard to figure out for a beginner, but there are numerous free tutorials available online.

Fonts

Study the fonts used on the covers in your book genre to get the feel for the current trends. Fonts are one of those elements of the book cover that should make the genre instantly clear to the readers. Easily recognizable types of fonts are used in the most popular genres, and there are also differences between the fonts used for fiction and non-fiction.

You can find free and affordable fonts on Google Fonts and Creative Market. If you subscribe for their newsletter, Creative Market will send you six free design goods every week, including free fonts. To install the fonts on your computer, download them, unzip them, and then right-click on the otf or ttf file. Select 'Install' and you're done.

Images

Make sure that whatever images you use are copyright free. There are numerous sources where you can get copyright free images, such as Unsplash, Pexels, and Pixabay, to name just a few.

The downside of such images, however, is that anyone else can use them too. You might thus want to edit and manipulate the image to make it look different. To some degree, you can do that in Snappa, but GIMP gives you even more options.

Images should convey the feel and general idea behind the story. They too are, like fonts, the main book cover element that should make the genre clear at the first glance. If you see a romantic couple on the cover, for example, you will instantly know what the book is about.

There are trends when it comes to how images on book covers and what kind of esthetics prevails. Study the images of other book covers in your genre to get the feel for current trends.

Design tips

Do not just take a cover template and a free stock image and simply plaster your title over it. Take the time to edit and adjust both the template and image to make them look unique. Avoid making the cover look like a template.

To make the book stand out in the crowd use bold colors and/or contrast. Go to Amazon and compare your cover with others to see how easy it would be to spot it. Make sure the title is readable and the image recognizable even at the small size.

Your name will not sell books unless you are famous, so it might not be a good idea to turn it into the main feature of the cover. Put the spotlight on the title for non-fiction and images for fiction instead.

17. BOOK DESCRIPTION

Book description has a similar role as a book cover – it should help the reader instantly understand the genre and book's content. Usually, this includes a hint of the plot that discloses just enough to make the reader want to know more but not enough to become a spoiler.

With book description, you are basically writing an ad for your book with the goal of selling it with a few well-written sentences. These should spur the reader's curiosity to the point of wanting to get the book.

Coming up with a good copy is an art very different from writing a book, and not an easy one to master either. While the story in a book unfolds over hundreds of pages, you only have a short paragraph or two for the book description.

What's more, you need different versions for various purposes:

- blurb
- logline
- ad copy and tagline
- copy for book promotion sites

Blurb

Blurb is a short book description used at the back of the book cover, in online bookstores, and on your website. It's usually comprised of two to three paragraphs and between 100 to 200 words long [34].

In addition to the description, blurb can include a short quote from a review or press as well as any notable credentials of the author, including best-selling status or awards.

Blurbs are meant to drive sales by not only making the readers curious about the book but also by mentioning any special achievements. They can include anything about the book or its author that could impress the reader.

Logline

Loglines are blurbs distilled into one or two sentences. Publishing houses, for instance, use them in their newsletters when promoting their latest books.

The idea is that the readers can learn enough from the logline to decide whether they want to know more. If they do, the link takes them to the product page where they find more information and can buy the book.

Logline can also be used when you are trying to find an agent or publisher for your book. Since we are all short on time, readers, agents, and publishers tend to make decisions fast and based on limited clues. Hence, the logline.

If the logline is convincing enough, we will click that link. Penguin Random House, for example, excels at writing such loglines. They will tell you everything you need to know in a second. Here is one such example from their newsletter:

Cottage by the Sea
By Debbie Macomber

A seaside town helps one young woman reclaim the light after darkness in a brand-new novel from #1 New York Times bestselling author Debbie Macomber [35].

From this sentence, you now know that the protagonist is a young woman, that something bad happened to her but she was able to find the way out, and that the story is set by the sea. You also learned that the book was written by a bestselling author.

From the logline in combination with the cover, we can safely assume that the genre is women's fiction, that this is likely a gentle and touching story with a happy ending that might include a bit of romance too. We got all this from a single sentence.

Here is another example for a book in a different genre, also by Penguin Random House:

Clear and Present Danger
By Tom Clancy

Jack Ryan gets caught in a war between the United States and a Colombian drug cartel and uncovers a shocking conspiracy [36].

Just from the longline, we can see that this book is an action thriller, we know who the protagonist is, what the plot is all about, and where it is happening.

As you can see from these examples, a well-written logline is more than enough for the reader to decide whether this might be the right book for them.

Ad copy and tagline

Ad copies and taglines are also short, one sentence statements about the book, but they are not the same thing as a logline and serve a different purpose. The main difference between ad copy and tagline on one side and logline on the other is placement.

Loglines are used in book-related settings, such as a publisher's newsletter or author's website where readers expect to see book-related content. Ad copy and taglines, on the other hand, are used in all other settings, such as social media.

Ad copy and taglines are focused either on the benefit of the book or serve as a hook. Since we devote far less attention to ads than other types of content, a tagline has to instantly grab our attention or it will not work at all.

While ad copy and tagline reveal something about the book, they are designed as catchy phrases rather than book descriptions. Like everything else in book promotion, though, this depends on the genre too.

For how-to and advice, focus on the benefits and how the book can change the reader's life for the better. For fiction and other types of non-fiction, come up with an intriguing line or a short quote instead.

Check the list of BookBub's best converting ads to see what kind of taglines and ad copy work well [37]. Here is one example from the list – a tagline from the ad for *The Trouble with Dukes* by Grace Burrowes:

"Smart, sexy, and oh-so romantic."

MARY BALOGH
New York Times bestselling author

This doesn't tell you anything about the plot or a protagonist, but it tells you everything you need to know about the nature of the book. In this case, a quote by a bestselling author was used as a tagline but this would be a good tagline even if it weren't a quote.

Here is another example from the same list for non-fiction, the ad copy for the book *10-Minute Mindfulness* by S.J. Scott and Barrie Davenport:

71 Simple Habits for Living in a Present Moment

The genre here is advice and how-to. The focus of the ad copy is thus on the benefits of the book and how it will help the reader.

Copy for book promotion sites

You will need to prepare yet another version of book description for book promotion sites and their newsletters (more on book promotion sites in Chapter 28). Some of these sites specifically request that a description must be different from the one on Amazon.

Using the same description first in the newsletter and then on the product page is counterproductive. When writing the copy for book promotion sites, place yourself in the shoes of the subscriber who receives the newsletter. The book description on Amazon should supplement what the reader already read in the newsletter and not just repeat it.

The length of book descriptions for book promotion sites differ too. Some of the sites only accept a short copy while others won't mind if you submit a much longer text. To know what to expect from each site, subscribe for their newsletter first.

Study the descriptions of other books in the genre to see which ones work best and why. Prepare two version of your book description – a shorter one for the sites with limited word count and a longer one for the rest of the book promotion sites.

18. AUTHOR BIO

Like with book description, you will also need different versions of your bio for the following purposes:

- a byline
- in your books
- on author pages
- on author website
- on book promotion sites

Byline

A good byline does for a writer what a good logline does for a book – it conveys the essence of the author's life and work in one or two sentences. Like loglines, though, these are not exactly easy to write.

To make it easier, you can use a simple formula – start with your name, state what you do and are good at, and finish with call to action. For instance:

> *Mateja is a self-published author whose latest book instantly became #1 New Release in several categories on Amazon. Visit Mateja's website matejaklaric.com to learn how you can make that happen too.*

Bylines are often placed at the end of guest blog posts. They usually include author's picture and links to their website or blog. Bylines are also used in social media profiles where space is limited, so that you have to present yourself with but a few words.

About the author

The content, placement, and length of author's bio in books depends on the type of the book. 'About the author' section is usually placed at the back of the book and includes a short biography.

With non-fiction, however, especially if you write about the topics that require certain credentials and expertise, you'll need to place this information at the front.

This isn't the same as 'About the author' and is often written as a part of introduction where you can also explain what led you write the book and why do you find sharing this information important.

Author pages

You'll need a short biography for your author pages on Amazon Author Central, Goodreads, Books2Read (Draft2Digital), and other book-related platforms. The length varies from author to author and there is no universally applicable recipe.

In general, though, these bios are not very long and range from only a couple of sentences to one or two paragraphs. The tone (e.g. serious vs. lighthearted) and content depends on the kind of books you write.

If you publish advice and how-to books, for instance, it's recommended to state your credentials and work experience. With fiction, you have more freedom and can mention your hobbies, indulgencies, or pets.

Author website and blog

The bio for your website or blog will depend on the platform you use. On Medium, for instance, you can barely squeeze a couple of sentences next to your profile picture, so you'll have to use a byline.

You can, of course, do whatever you want on your own website. Authors usually use a classic 'About' page that includes a picture and a few paragraphs about the author. For that, you can use the same bio as on author pages. I see it as a nice touch, though, when writers make the bio on their website a bit different and more personal.

19. PRICE POINT

Finding the right price point for the book is highly important for sales. It's good to remember that this has little to do with how much you think the book is worth based on the time, money, and effort you invested in it, and everything with how much you can sell it for.

Book prices depend on the length, topic, competition, and trends on the market. Longer books, for instance, are more expensive than short stories. Books that focus on a rare topic can also be more expensive than the books in popular genres where the prices tend to drop because of the competition.

If your book includes illustrations or artwork, this may justify a higher price. As for the trends on the market, they are about how much readers on average spend on books, what is currently in demand, and at what price point books sell best.

Finding this data, however, can be hard. Big players and agencies have years of experience and access to professional reports and analytics. As a new writer on the block, you have none of that, so you'll have to find reliable information elsewhere.

How to find and evaluate the data

Some book promotion sites and distribution platforms occasionally disclose a part of their data to help writers set the right price for their books. While this is helpful, it needs to be taken with some caution and properly evaluated.

The problem is that the data these distributors and book services share is limited to their user base and thus cannot be generalized across the whole book market. Written Word Media, for instance, is one of the most reliable and trustworthy book promotion platforms but their report is based on their userbase and not all readers.

Book promotion services are all about discounted or lower-priced books. Their readers are thus not only interested in finding new books but are also looking for bargains. It is thus not surprising that according to the Written Word Media ebooks sell best at $0.99 [38].

It's safe to assume that this would be the case on other book promotion sites as well. And indeed, when you order a book promotion, these sites will either suggest that you offer your book at a discounted price or will not even promote your book unless it's free or discounted.

This, however, doesn't necessarily mean that books priced at $0.99 in general sell best and that you should set the price that low without considering other factors as well. As the Written Word Media report also points out, selling a lot of books don't necessarily translate into the highest earnings as well.

According to the report, the books that were priced at $3.99 sold fewer copies but generated the highest revenue. So that too is something to consider when setting the price. Keep in mind that your royalties on Amazon will be only 35% for books priced at less than $2.99. By raising the price to $2.99, you'll earn twice as much (70%) from each sale.

As another example, Smashwords' 2017 yearly report [7] stated that the most common price point for indie books was

$2.99, but the price points that maximized the sales were $3.99, $4.99, $0.99, and $2.99 – in that order. So, the cheapest books don't necessarily lead to more sales and they certainly don't lead to the highest revenue.

Still, this is statistics – the average book prices that include a whole range of different genres. Coming up with the right price for your specific book will depend on many factors. Fast and easy reads in competitive genres such as romance, for instance, sell at lower prices.

The average price across the genres is thus of no use. At the very least, you need to know what's the average price in your genre and category. Knowing what's the median price, however, would be even more reliable.

The good news is – you can have that and more with Kindle Ranker [39], an affordable app that helps you set the price point for your book, estimate the earning potential, and find best categories for your book.

Kindle Ranker uses data from Amazon, but since that's where by far the most book sales take place, this will give you a good enough estimation of the price ranges to apply it to other platforms as well.

Free ebook offers

According to the previously mentioned Smashwords' report [7], the popularity of free books is decreasing with every passing year, but they still get more downloads than the ones readers have to pay for. Just giving a book away without knowing what exactly you want to achieve by this, however, will likely not lead to desired results. Free ebooks only make sense when you want to:

- get more reviews,
- promote the first book in a series,
- build a platform.

Getting more reviews

Offering your ebook for free might indeed lead to more reviews. On the other hand, though, you also risk getting more bad reviews. It's not clear why this happens and why this strategy can be a two-edged sword.

It might have something to do with the perceived value of books that are available for free. The readers might subconsciously think they are of lesser quality than they truly are. But also, many readers download free books just because they are free and not because they understand or are interested in the genre.

Promoting a series

Promoting a series by offering the first book for free is a strategy that makes the most sense and can be highly efficient. Since buying books by unknown self-published authors is seen as a risk, you can solve this problem by giving the readers the first one for free.

This works much like product testers in stores. The only downside of this is that you need to publish several books in the series for this to work. If you have just started out with the first book, you'll obviously not be able to do it.

Building a platform

Some writers claim that putting their ebooks on permafree did wonders for their email list. I cannot confirm that based on my personal experience. That is not to say, however, that these claims aren't true, it's just that they cannot be generalized.

There are cheaper and easier ways to build your email list. As stated earlier, the appeal of free ebooks is wearing off and the downloads have been steadily declining for years. Giving away books for free is far less efficient than it used to be and will likely be even less so in the future.

Also, like with series, this option could work better if you have many published books and offer one of them for free. But for a self-published beginner with only one or two published books, this will likely not lead to the results you are hoping for.

Free ebooks on Amazon

You can easily change your book's price to zero on distribution platforms such as Draft2Digital but offering your ebooks for free is not that easy on Amazon KDP. Amazon KDP gives you two options for free ebooks – KDP Select and Match Price.

KDP Select

When you publish on Amazon KDP, you can choose to enroll the ebook in KDP Select. This means that you will be only allowed to sell your ebook on Amazon and nowhere else, including your website, for the duration of 90 days.

Among the benefits you get in return is a Free Promotion option. This, however, limits the days you can have your ebook available for free to 5 days during each 90-day period. The question is, are these limited options and restrictions worth it? If you decide against it, Match Price is another option.

Match Price

To be able to use the Match Price option, your ebook has to be available for free on other platforms first. Set the price of your book to zero on Apple or Kobo, copy the link that proves the book is free, and then contact Amazon KDP support and ask them to match the price.

You will find this option in the Help section on your Amazon KDP dashboard. Click 'Help' and find 'Contact us' button in the lower left corner. Click it and select 'Amazon Product Page' from the list of options. You will see 'Price Matching' among the options. Select it, fill in the details and submit.

With Match Price, you can have your ebook available for free for as long as you want. Since there is no limit, this option is the one to choose when you want to set the first book in the series on permafree.

20. PREORDERS

Preorders are a great way to boost your books rank even before it gets published. The more sales you get during the preorder period, the higher the book's rank before and after it gets published.

Higher rank, among other things, means that your book will get more exposure and with that a chance for more sales. But there is one thing you need to be careful with – your manuscript has to be ready by the deadline.

Different platforms have different rules, though. On Draft2Digital, you can set up a preorder with no manuscript for up to a year in advance. On Amazon, on the other hand, you cannot set up a preorder without a manuscript and also for no more than 90 days in advance.

If you have a problem with sticking to deadlines, avoid preorders on Amazon. While you can change the publishing date on Draft2Digital if needed, there is no such option on Amazon. And if you cancel the preorder, Amazon won't let you use it again for a whole year.

I've seen books that were available for preorder but were unfinished drafts when published. That doesn't look good and you risk getting poor reviews. Be aware that you will have to upload the final version of your manuscript at least a couple of days before the official publishing date.

21. CATEGORIES & KEYWORDS

When publishing on self-publishing platforms, you have to select keywords and categories for your book. This may sound easy and straight-forward enough but actually isn't.

Some categories are a lot more competitive than others and if you place your book in the less crowded ones instead, the book stands a better chance of getting into the top 100 in the category.

That alone can improve the sales. With the right selection of keywords, you can additionally increase the visibility of your book in search results on the platform. This can have a positive impact on the sales too.

Categories

Amazon KDP lets you select only two categories on your dashboard, and thus many writers don't know that you can have your book listed in 10 categories. You ll have to contact Amazon customer service and ask them to add your book to the additional eight categories, though.

To do that, go to the Help section on your KDP dashboard and find the 'Contact us' button at the bottom of the column on the left. Click it and then select 'Book details.' This will open a new list of options. Select 'Update Categories and Keywords.'

You will need the book's ASIN number and the list of desired categories ready. But how do you select these categories and how do you know in which ones your book stands the best chance of rising to the top? This is where the previously mentioned Kindle Ranker [39] comes in.

Kindle Ranker

There are several apps that can help you find the best categories on Amazon, such as KDP Rocket and K-lytics. The prices for these, however, are rather steep for a self-published writer on a budget.

Also, if you haven't published many books, it will not be cost-efficient to invest that much into this, since only adjusting your categories will not be enough to turn your book into a best-seller.

Kindle Ranker is a good alternative since you can use it for free for up to two queries per day or purchase an unlimited weekly pass for $2 (at the time of writing this book), which is much more affordable than other apps on the market.

The app will give you all the information you need about the competition, including the median prices of the books in your genre and category. You will also be able to copy the selected category strings and paste them in your request to Amazon KDP's customer service.

Kindle Ranker will provide you with information on how many books per day you'd need to sell to get to the top in each category. In addition, you will find out what is the estimated earning potential in each category.

Keywords

You also need to provide keywords related to your book. The best keywords are not single words, but phrases and strings of words readers use when they search for books. In the case of this book, for example, I used 'book marketing for authors' as one of the so-called long-tail keywords.

It's hard to guess what people might be looking for and what phrases they use in their searches. Instead of guessing, go to Amazon and type in the keywords related to your book as if you were searching for books similar to yours. Amazon's autocomplete search feature will give you a list of suggestions. You can then use these as long-tail keywords.

22. REVIEWS

Your book can get different types of reviews: directly from the readers, from book bloggers, and in the media specialized in books. You can also buy an editorial review or get a blurb from a well-known writer or expert.

The latter, however, are hard to get if you are a newly self-published author with no agent and publishing contract. Editorial reviews also cost a fortune and might not be worth the investment [40].

As for the media and best-selling authors, they are overflown with such requests. Unless your book is extraordinary or covers a topic of great interest, it will be very hard to get their attention.

Readers' reviews

Some platforms sell readers' reviews. Do not use them, for paying for readers' reviews is against the rules on Amazon. What you want above all are honest reviews from the real readers who purchased your book.

There are several reasons for this. To begin with, when the reader buys the book on Amazon, 'Verified purchase' appears next to the review, which gives it more credibility. Some online stores even delete the reviews unless the reviewer bought the book there.

Real reviews also sound sincere and convincing. But most importantly, you want to know what your readers truly thought about the book. As a writer, you need feedback and that's another reason why you shouldn't buy or swap the reviews.

It's also important to know, though, that only a small percentage of readers leave reviews. Out of more than thousand readers who downloaded my book *How to Self-Publish Your Book: The Fast, Free & Easy Way*, for instance, only 14 left a review. That's roughly 1.5%.

This is normal for a self-published writer who doesn't have a huge following and a lot of published books yet, and it became even more normal since the Amazon's new rules prevent the readers who don't spend enough money on Amazon from posting reviews.

Amazon's review rules

Since so many authors abused the reviews and there was a flood of fake ones, Amazon fought back by adjusting the rules. Amazon is above all concerned with customers' satisfaction and that's why it wants a reliable and honest feedback on the products it sells.

In addition to banning bought reviews, the new rules now prevent those who don't spend at least $50 per year on Amazon from posting reviews, which is a matter of much controversy [41]. Amazon removed a lot of existing reviews and will likely continue to do so in the future. To prevent having your book reviews removed, stick to the Amazon's rules:

Do this:

- offer your books for free or at a discount to increase the number of downloads
- ask the reader to leave a review in the book
- offer advanced review copies

You can also try to get reviews on websites such as The Kindle Book Review [42] that connect writers with book reviewers for free. This option doesn't guarantee reviews, though.

Do NOT do this:

- do not buy or offer an incentive in exchange for a review (this includes review swapping and offering free bonus content or services)
- do not let book bloggers who use affiliate links to books post the review of your book on Amazon – affiliate links are also an incentive
- do not ask family and friends for reviews

Check Amazon's Community Guidelines for details on their review policy [43].

Book blog reviews

It's highly unlikely that your book will be picked by the media, but you can try and get it reviewed by book bloggers. Many bloggers do this either for fun or business and then publish the reviews on their blogs and social media accounts.

In addition to the previously mentioned The Kindle Book Review [42], there are websites and apps, such as Book Sirens and Reedsy Tools that can help you find all sorts of book reviewers fast and easy, so that you don't have to spend hours on Google trying to find the right fit for your book.

Do not use the main Book Sirens site for authors, though because that's where they charge for reviews. Use their Book Reviewers Directory [44] instead. That's a free app that helps you find book bloggers. You can filter the list of blogs by genre, whether the blogger cross-post the reviews on Goodreads and social media, and also whether the blogger even reviews self-published books.

Another option is a free book blogger finder on Reedsy Tools [45]. It works much like Book Sirens' but with fewer options. On Reedsy Tools, you have another tool called Book Tool Channel Guide [46]. That's where you can find bloggers who review books on YouTube.

23. THE COST OF PROMOTION

So far, we have covered free promotion options, but these will not be enough. For fast growth, you'll have to invest in paid promotion too. But how much does this cost? A short answer would be as much or as little as you are willing and able to invest.

The results, however, will also reflect that. The lower the budget, the longer it will take for your books to get noticed. Successful self-published writers thus keep investing a lot into promotion and keep building a following.

Mark Dawson, one of the Amazon KDP's self-publishing superstars, for instance, spends about 10% of his income on promotion. Given his impressive earnings, that would be about $8,000 per month. Dawson is quite capable of investing $400 per day in Facebook ads alone [47].

As another example, Derek Murphy, another self-published author, excels at building his email list. He used a unique approach of top-notch giveaways and offered a free writing retreat in a European castle. This wasn't cheap either, but it was so interesting that it got him free press coverage on CCN [48].

And then there is a romance superstar Meredith Wild who managed to build an empire with her self-publishing business and now runs her own publishing company. How did she do it?

To begin with, Wild majored in English but also has a strong entrepreneurial background in marketing and design. She and her husband raised and borrowed enough capital to invest in a six figures marketing campaign for her first book that even included running expensive movie theatre ads [49].

Success, as you can see from these examples, is never accidental. Best-selling writers regularly invest in promotion and devote a significant part of their income to it. You'll have to invest too but expect to spend more than you'll earn at the beginning.

Like any other business, self-publishing requires a big investment at the beginning to get it off the ground. The good news, however, is that while spending lots of money certainly helps, it's also not the only way to get at least some results.

I could, for instance, only afford to nvest a couple hundred dollars but have nevertheless managed to repeatedly get my books to #1 in several categories on Amazon. The book that you are reading now became a #1 New Release in several categories on Amazon as soon as I launched a preorder, and then turned into a #1 Best Seller – all of this without any reviews yet.

But the key to making a profit and not just getting your book to the top of a category is finding cost-effective options and avoiding burning money on things that don't work. That's why traditional publishers use the so-called book P&L (profit & loss) sheets.

They use it to evaluate the risk and potential for profit before making a final decision on whether to publish a book or not.

24. PROFIT & LOSS

One of the main things traditional publishers rely on when creating a P&L sheet are years of experience and in-depth knowledge of the market. As a newly self-published writer who has just started building their self-publishing career, you don't have that yet.

What's more, while you are walking in the dark not knowing what to expect, even traditional publishers with all the resources and experience often invest in books that flop and don't bring a return on investment. Still, they do what they can to prevent that, and so should you.

Creating P&L sheet

P&L sheets are basically balance sheets that estimate the potential for profit and loss when publishing a certain book. Calculating this is much easier for a traditional publisher since they are dealing with fewer unknowns.

They, for instance, know exactly how much book production and promotion cost, and what kind of price point would be realistic. Based on the experience, they also know how well books in various genres sell. They can thus make an educated guess about the book's potential for financial success [50].

You don't have these advantages, but you can still create a P&L for your book. If you only plan on self-publishing your paperback on Amazon KDP, for instance, you won't have to invest anything in the print edition, since Amazon KDP is a print-on-demand service.

You can also format the book yourself and save some money there too. For step-by-step instructions on how to do that, refer to the first book in this series – *How to Self-Publish Your Book: The Fast, Free & Easy Way* [51].

You might need to invest in proofreading, editing, and book cover, though, but the main cost of your self-publishing project will be book promotion. Especially if you don't have a platform yet and want to sell more than a few copies, that is the one cost you won't be able to avoid.

The main question thus is, how much are you going to invest and what can you expect to get back. To be able to estimate that, you will first need to determine the realistic price point and then estimate the sales.

If you haven't yet set the price point for your book, go to Chapter 19 and take care of that first. Your royalties will depend on the price, and you need this information so that you can estimate the earnings.

Estimating your book's sales

The question is, how can you predict the sales when you have no previous record to rely on? Since no one collects this information for self-published authors in an organized manner, and distribution platforms do not disclose this information, this can be a challenge.

It's hard to find the latest and thus most relevant numbers. In general, though, the reported sales for the self-publishing debut range from less than 100 to 500 in lifetime sales. These are more educated guesses than rock-solid facts, but when I compare them to the sales of my books, they make sense.

I sold 115 copies of my first book and 343 copies of my second book in the first year, and both keep selling. As for the one you are reading now, I've already sold close to 200 copies while it was only available for preorder.

I have not yet managed to make a profit with any of my books, though. The reason for this is that I gave away hundreds of books for free and had to sell at low price points to boost the ranks and build the following. I thus had to accept low royalties.

But this is a normal part of the process. It on average takes from five to ten self-published books before one reaches the turning point and starts making a profit [52]. The more books you publish, the bigger your following, and the bigger your following, the more sales you can make.

You need to consider other factors that affect the sales too, such as the popularity of the genre, how good you are at marketing and promotion, and how much you can afford to invest. None of my books fall into a popular genre and I self-published on a budget, which makes my results pretty good. The numbers are growing, and I know it will just take a bit more time.

Take the sales numbers reported by other writers as an estimate that can help you understand the rather harsh reality of self-publishing and publishing industry in general. Also, keep in mind that sales do not necessarily also translate into profit.

As you can see from these numbers, most self-published writers suffer a loss with their first book(s). Especially if you are doing this on a budget, it will take a couple of years and several self-published books before you can expect to generate an income.

25. WHY BOOKS DON'T SELL

There are numerous possible reasons for low sales, and if you haven't achieved the desired results, you have to try to figure out what is the problem. We have mentioned most of these so far but let's make a list to make it clearer. The most common reasons for low sales are:

- no platform
- unpopular genre
- poor book cover and/or description
- undefined audience
- bad reviews
- low budget

If you have no platform yet, this will be reflected in your book sales and that's why you need to build a platform first and foremost. But the genre can add a lot to this problem. Not all types of books are in high demand. Use Kindle Ranker [39] to estimate the selling potential of your book's category and genre.

You also have a problem if your book doesn't fit well into any genre. As stated at the beginning of this book, the more unusual the book, the harder and more expensive it will be to find the right audience. In this case, focus on growing and cultivating your highly specific audience first.

Poor book cover and description are often the reason for low sales. A cover says a lot about the book, or at least it should say a lot about the book. Poorly designed cover that screams 'amateur' will give an impression that the book is equally poorly written. Add to this a description that fails to entice or doesn't clearly show the benefits of your book, and you have low sales.

Poorly defined, misdefined, or too broadly defined audience is another common reason why books don't sell. In the case of this book, for instance, I improved the results simply by making it clear that the book was written for writers *on a budget*. By narrowing down your target audience, you can achieve better results.

Bad reviews usually mean that your book didn't meet the standards of the readers. This could be due to poor writing or the lack of editing. You can, however, also get bad reviews because the readers didn't agree with your point of view.

Sometimes books sell well despite the bad reviews, but that's an exception rather than the rule. The best way to avoid having such problems is to only publish your best and polished work so that the book gets enough good reviews to mitigate the consequences of any poor ones.

On the good note, though, many buyers even prefer to see a couple of bad reviews among the good ones, for it can be expected that not everyone will like the book, and this makes the ratings seem more realistic.

You can have a great book, cover, description, and well-defined audience, but none of this will be enough if you don't also have a high enough budget to promote and get your book in front of the readers.

The best way to solve this problem is to throw yourself head-on into free activities that can help you get your work out there, such as blogging, guest blogging, publishing in publications, being active on social media, and trying to have your book reviewed by book bloggers.

The buyer's journey

The buyer's journey represents the stages a buyer goes through when deciding whether to buy a certain product or not. This is not specific to the publishing industry, but the same principles can nevertheless be applied to book sales.

You can use the buyer's journey to determine at which point of the journey you are losing sales so that you can make corrections and improve the results. The journey has three stages: awareness, consideration, and decision. In addition to these, a post-purchase phase is also important.

Awareness

In the first stage of the journey, a buyer becomes aware of a problem or need. In the case of how-to or self-help books, for instance, the buyer could be looking for a book with a solution to their problem. In the case of fiction, the book could satisfy a desire for entertainment or excitement.

Consider what kind of problem or need your book addresses. Is this something a lot of people might be looking for? Also, who exactly are these people who'd need this kind of book and where could you find them? You've guessed it – this stage is all about defining and narrowing down your audience well.

Consideration

At this stage, the buyer starts looking for a solution and evaluates various options. Applied to books, that would mean looking for the best book that could satisfy their need.

On the book market, there is a huge selection of possible choices and if the buyer misses your book, the chance for making a sale is gone.

How can a buyer miss your book? The answer could be the lack of promotion or poor targeting. Alternatively, they might have never noticed the book because the cover was too inconspicuous and easy to miss among many other books.

Even if the buyer notices the book, however, this still doesn't mean that they will check it out as well. Let's say that your book appears in an ad and that the book cover, ad copy, and price are all interesting enough for the buyer to click on the link. Congrats – your book made it to the next stage of the journey.

If your ad got no clicks, though, but you are sure that you promoted it in all the right places and to the right audience, consider the book's cover, description, and price again. Is there a room for improvement?

Decision

The reader who clicked the ad is now investigating your book's page on Amazon looking for additional information. Here, they are likely to read the book's description, look inside the book, check the reviews, rank, price, and author's bio before making the final decision.

Providing that all these factors satisfy the reader and convince them that the book will be interesting and useful (all of which should ideally be confirmed by the reviews and sales rank), they might decide to buy.

But if no one buys your book even though many clicked the ad, then look for the problem on the product page. The problem could be the reviews, the description, your bio or a combination of these.

Post-purchase phase

After the reader finishes reading the book, there are three possibilities of what could happen – first, the reader loved the book, second, the reader neither loved nor hated the book, and third, the reader hated the book.

In the first case, the reader will likely leave a glowing review and recommend your book to others. In the second case, the reader might not even bother to leave a review. In the last case, the reader will likely leave a devastating review and warn other people about it too.

Bottom line – no amount of book promotion will be of any use if the book isn't something the readers are interested in or if it doesn't meet their expectations. If, however, you deliver, the readers will reward you by spreading the word and promoting your work.

26. MEASURE THE RESULTS

Book promotion is a trial and error process. You will have to experiment and try different approaches to find what works best for your book. You will also have to be able to identify and address any issues mentioned in the previous chapter so that you can fix them.

Statistics and analytics are your best friends because they help you measure and understand the results of your activities. If you are not already using the following tools, become familiar with them and start using them now:

- Website and blog stats
- Sales and author rank
- Book promotion sites stats
- Paid ads stats

Website and blog stats

Turn checking your blog and website statistics into a habit. Only some blogging platforms, though, make that possible. Medium, for instance, has a pretty neat stats page, while on other platforms, such as Tumblr, you have to connect Google Analytics [53].

Most website builders, such as Squarespace or Weebly, offer a basic insight into the number of visitors and clicks. This, however, might depend upon the plan you choose. Usually, you can also connect the website to Google Analytics, which is a good option but takes some learning.

Having access to statistics allows you to see which of your stories and posts brought you the most visitors and what kind of content is of interest to your readers. It also helps you track where the traffic came from so that you can see which social media or guest posts lead to the best results.

For a beginner, your basic website or blog stats might suffice for the purpose. But if you don't have access to it or would like to have a more in-depth insight (which is recommended), learn how to use Google Analytics.

Sales and author rank

Amazon KDP dashboard lets you monitor your ebook sales in real time. When it comes to paperback sales, though, these will only show after the book was already shipped. You can thus only see how efficient your promotion campaigns by monitoring the ebook sales on Amazon.

If you also publish through a distribution platform, such as Draft2Digital, you also won't be able to track the sales in real-time since the distributor needs to wait for the reports from each of the sales channels before they can send them to you.

Amazon has another benefit when it comes to monitoring the results – Amazon Author Central lets you monitor your books' and author rank. You will see how your book rank in comparison with other books on Amazon and how you rank as an author in comparison with other authors on Amazon.

Having this information will help you keep things in perspective. Currently, there are about 6 million ebooks available on Amazon, in addition to about ten times as many print books [54]. Amazon doesn't disclose these numbers, though, and new books are being published daily, so take these numbers as estimates.

You might feel bad if your ebook 'only' ranks among the top 300,000 but given these numbers that would mean that it is in the top 5% of all ebooks on Amazon. Be aware that the number of books on Amazon is huge and keeps growing daily.

You might be surprised how relatively few sales it takes to get your book into the top 5%. On the other hand, though, it's extremely hard to get and keep your book in the top 0,1%, which is where the books start to generate big revenues.

Paid ads stats

When you place paid ads, you also get insight into the analytics so that you can monitor the ads' performance. This can be complex in the case of Facebook but less so when you advertise on Amazon or Goodreads.

It's important that you understand these reports and know how to read the dashboard so that you can adjust the strategy when needed. That's why you need to become familiar with the basic terms used on these dashboards.

Impressions / views

The terms impressions and views are interchangeable. They tell you how many times your ad was shown to the users on the platform.

Frequency

On Facebook's advertising dashboards, you will also have Frequency. Frequency stands for the number of times the same person saw your ad. Frequency of 1 thus means that each user saw your ad only once. A higher frequency is desirable due to the Rule of 7 but it costs more since you will have to run the ad longer to achieve it.

Clicks

Clicks tell you how many times the users clicked on your ad. This information tells you how efficient is your ad and lets you calculate the CTR and conversion rate.

CTR

CTR stands for Click Through Rate and it's expressed as a percentage of those who have not only seen the ad but also responded by clicking on it. CTR 0.5%, for instance, means that out of 1000 people who saw the ad, 5 people clicked on it.

An average CTR on Goodreads ranges from 0.05% to 0.5% and it's safe to assume that this goes for other book-related platforms as well. It's not unusual for CTR to be even lower than 0.05%, and if it's higher than 0.5%, that's an excellent result.

CTR depends on a combination of the product (readers' interest), ad (efficiency), and targeting (reaching the right audience). On some platforms, targeting is highly limited and that alone can make it very hard to achieve a good CTR.

Conversion rate

A conversion rate is a percentage of those who have not only clicked the ad but also bought your book. A good conversion rate is much higher than CTR. It can be well over 10% and even as much as 50%.

This is because those who have clicked the ad were already interested in the book. If your ad gets clicks but doesn't convert well, check your book's product page for the possible cause.

CPC & CPM

When you place an ad, you can sometimes choose whether you want to pay per click or per impressions. CPC stands for cost per click and CPM stands for cost per thousand impressions (or views).

For books sales, it's better to select CPC – you want to pay for the clicks because these lead to sales. With CPM, you will have to pay for the views regardless of whether anyone clicked on the ad and bought the book or not.

This is even more so on the platforms where you have limited targeting options that only make it possible to target broadly. You certainly don't want to pay for the views if you cannot even target your potential readers well.

Bidding and auction

You are competing with other ads in what is basically an auction for the limited advertising space and that's why you must bid. A bid is how much you are willing to pay per click (CPC) or per thousand impressions (CPM), depending on which option you chose.

The ads with higher bids stand a better chance of being displayed. Most platforms will suggest the bid based on the average bid at the time when you place an ad, so you won't have to guess.

If you bid too low, your ad might not show at all so that's not recommended. But when your bid is higher than average, you might even pay less than what you bid, since the final price depends on other people's bids.

ROI

ROI stands for return on investment and is expressed as a percentage. You can calculate it to see whether your investment in book promotion resulted in returns or loss. You can use an online ROI calculator [55] or calculate it yourself by using the following formula:

(royalties − cost of promotion)/cost of promotion*100 = ROI (expressed in %)

Amazon Advertising

Amazon Advertising dashboard only gives you a few basic pieces of information, such as the number of impressions and CPC. You will even have to calculate CTR yourself. To calculate CTR, use the following formula:

number of clicks/number of impressions*100 = CTR (expressed in %)

There is also a unique metrics Amazon s using and that might baffle you – AcoS (Advertising Cost of Sales). This is the Amazon's version of ROI that uses the book's price and cost of promotion to calculate the return on investment. Since your actual earnings (royalties) will be lower, though, you have to take that into account when interpreting it.

To break even, for instance, the campaign's AcoS should be equal to your royalties. If your royalties are 35% of the book's price, then AcoS should also be 35% and if your royalties are 70%, then AcoS should also be 70%. Anything higher than that means that you are spending more than what you'll earn in royalties.

27. BOOK PROMOTION SITES

Book promotion sites are unique to the publishing industry. They have large email lists of subscribers and charge to promote books in their newsletters. Their readers are, for the most part, interested in getting a good deal on books.

These sites thus only promote free or discounted books priced below $2.99 or at the most $3.99. Many of them also use affiliate links. This means that they earn a commission from the sales in addition to what they charge the writers for promotion.

It's thus in their interest to generate as many sales as possible, and that's why many of them have strict policies regarding what kind of books they accept. Most of the best ones will only promote books that already have reviews with an average of above three stars.

Recommended sites

Promotion on book promotion sites can lead to quick sales and that's why traditional publishers and self-published writers use them. They can, however, also be tricky since not all of them are cost-efficient and trustworthy. It's thus recommended to check their ratings on Reedsy before placing an order.

Reedsy's list of book promotion sites

You can find a list or promotion sites on Reedsy's blog [56]. Reedsy rated these services based on the reports by writers, so these ratings are not 100% reliable and applicable to all kind of books and genres. For the most part, however, I can agree with the ratings given my experience with these sites.

You can filter the Reedsy's list by the site's rating (tier), genre, and price. To be on the safe side, only trust the sites that made it to the Tiers I and II (four and five stars) and avoid the rest.

In addition, also check the review of self-publishing services by the Alliance of Independent Authors that also includes book promotion sites [57]. There are many shady businesses in self-publishing industry and the review can help you avoid them.

BookBub

BookBub is a superstar among book promotion sites. It became close to impossible to get your book promoted in their newsletter, though, since they only accept a tiny fraction of submitted books. Lately, these tend to be traditionally published best-sellers.

You can, however, order a paid ad for your book in their newsletter through their BookBub Partners program [58]. BookBub has a lot of useful resources for writers and a blog with tips and advice [59]. Subscribing to their newsletter and creating an author page is recommended.

Policies

Many of the best book promotion sites only accept books that already have at least five and sometimes at least ten positive reviews. Some sites require an average of at least four stars, while others are willing to accept books with an average of three stars.

Some websites also promote books with no reviews if these are new releases. Not all, however, accept books available for preorder. And then there can be a minimum word count limit too since some won't promote short stories and novellas.

Many also won't let you promote the same book too often and a certain number of weeks or even months must pass before you can promote again. Some of the platforms only promote free ebooks, others are specialized in the most popular genres.

Since these websites are owned by different people, their policies vary to a significant degree. You'll thus have to be well organized and keep track of all these rules when you run a campaign on different sites.

The best sites are usually also booked weeks in advance, so you'll have to schedule the promotion ahead of time. It's best to create an Excel sheet to keep the dates and cost under control as well as track the results. You need to know how many sales each of these sites brought.

Cost

Just like their policies, the prices vary as well. They range from highly affordable to extremely expensive. You can order a promotion for a few dollars on one site and for hundreds on another. The price, however, might not reflect the value and expected results of the promotion.

Don't be afraid to complain and voice your concerns if the promotion on the sites with steep prices resulted in lower or equal number of sales than what you got on the sites that charge much less. If there were no results, ask for a refund.

Run a promotion on a few sites first, though, so that you can compare the results and exclude the fault of your own, such as a poor book cover or description. If you had good results with the same book cover and description on some sites but not on others, you can be sure that the problem is the site and not your book.

Quality book promotion sites have a vetting process in place and will refuse to promote the books that don't meet their standards or that would be of no interest to their readers. Good book promotion sites will help you get results and not just take your money and run.

Subscribe for special offers

It's recommended to subscribe to these sites' newsletters as both a reader and an author. That's how you'll stay in the know as well as be notified when the site offers a discount on book promotion. As a writer on a budget, be on the lookout for such opportunities since they can save you quite a lot on campaigns.

Results

Unless you by some miracle manage to get your book in the BookBub's newsletter, don't expect hundreds of sales, and maybe not even tens. Still, the results of these campaigns will likely be better than what you could achieve on a limited budget with social media ads. This is where you can reach the readers who are looking for new books.

On the downsides, though, most book promotion sites don't share their analytics. You will thus have no idea how many people saw your book and how many clicked on it. All you will be able to see is the number of ebook sales on your Amazon KDP dashboard.

This makes it very hard to pinpoint at which stage you might be losing sales and why. Be aware that even if these sites indeed have as many subscribers as they claim, that doesn't tell you anything about the quality of their email lists and social media accounts.

You cannot know many of these subscribers and followers are active readers who care to open these emails. Among the rare few that offer valuable insight into what you can expect in terms of clicks and sales are Ebook Hounds and Genre Pulse.

Ebook Hounds

You'll find the number of average downloads of the promoted books on Ebook Hounds [60]. These differ for free and paid book as well as the genre, so don't take the statement at the top of the page on how this author got over 200 sales as a norm.

You will see from the numbers below this quote that what you can really expect is to get from 12 to 560 downloads for free ebooks, and from 4 to 125 sales for paid ebooks. This will depend on the genre, and the most popular genre on Ebook Hounds is mystery.

Genre Pulse

Genre Pulse [61] is another book promotion site that gives you some insight into how many clicks not only yours but also the books of other authors received. Getting there, however, is a bit more complicated and takes some work.

You have to add */stats* to the *genrepulse.com* URL, to find this information for all the books they promoted [62]. A bit.ly URL next to each book is what you need to copy and paste in your browser to see the results. If you want to learn more about the books, you will then also have to copy and paste the link to the book on Amazon. It's located just above the bit.ly URL on the book's stats page.

You can use this information to see how books in different genres and at different price points are doing. That's how you can predict how many clicks you can expect from your campaign given the genre.

Check everything twice

You need to be extra careful with book promotion platforms and check everything twice, from whether you are being charged correctly to whether the book campaign ran or not.

It's best to create an Excel sheet and write down what exactly you ordered, when you ordered it, how much it should cost, what was included in the package, and on what day the promotion should run.

Check that the numbers and dates ad up before you pay and then make sure to check whether the book was included in the newsletter. It happened to me that the book promotion platform didn't run my ad since they somehow missed my payment. Don't be afraid to ask questions and request a refund if needed.

What to avoid

Only promote on book promotion sites that charge based on a genre and pay using PayPal account. Using PayPal makes settling any disputes easier and you stand a better chance of getting a refund if needed.

Especially if you have a book in a less popular genre, avoid costly one-price-for-all sites. You will likely be disappointed in the results, since this might be good for popular genres, but is way overpriced for others.

Also, don't pay for apps that submit your book to free book promotion sites. Most of the books submitted for free promotion never get promoted – app or no app. Even if you get lucky and have your book featured on one of these free sites, the results are usually not worth paying for.

28. PAID ADS

There are two types of platforms that offer paid ads: book related platforms (Amazon, Goodreads, and BookBub) and social media (e.g. Facebook and Instagram).

The results are in both cases unpredictable. This is not so only because one needs a great ad to which the readers respond well, but also because these platforms are based on the system of bids.

Only ads with the highest bids will get in front of the public. But that alone is not enough. Unless your ads also generate a lot of clicks, they might not be displayed as often or even at all. While this won't cost a dime, it will also not bring any results.

You'll thus need to experiment and keep placing new and improved ads, go higher with your bid, and try to come up with a great copy. But that won't help if you won't also be able to target the right audience and on some platforms that can be hard.

There are quite a few differences between book platforms and social media. It's important to understand these so that you can come up with the best strategy for each platform.

Book platforms vs. social media

The main differences between these two types of advertising platforms are the users, targeting options, cost, and available ad types. There are benefits and downsides to both, so let's take a closer look at these.

Users & targeting

The users you find on book platforms are exactly what you need – people who are actively looking for books. You don't want to miss the opportunity of presenting your books to them.

Social media, on the other hand, are a completely different story. Almost everybody uses them, including many of those who couldn't care less about books. This means that you'll have to target really well.

Targeting options on book platforms are much more basic than on social media. While you want to narrow down your audience as much as possible and get your book in front of a highly specific group of readers, book platforms can make that hard for some genres.

On book platforms, you can only target based on the genre, keywords, or similar authors and the list of available genres only includes the most popular ones. To a limited degree, you can also target based on location.

Targeting on social media, on the other hand, can be much more nuanced. You can target by age, location, and all sorts of interests in addition to genre and keywords. This can work better for niche books.

Cost

One of the major downsides of advertising on social media is the high price. The bids just keep rising and are getting quite high comparing to book platforms. You can also only pay per click on book platforms, while social media usually charge per impressions.

Paying per click is much better for a writer on a budget since you can get your book in front of thousands of readers without having to pay a dime unless someone also clicks on the ad. Because only those who click might also buy the book, paying per click is what you want.

As good as this sounds, though, there is a caveat – the competition on these platforms is so intense that it might be impossible to spend even a fraction of your budget because your ads might not be displayed all that much or might not have a good CTR.

It can be hard to spend money on book platforms, but you can get broke easily on social media platforms. These platforms will keep displaying your ads for as long as you can afford to pay the high bids, but that can soon become very expensive and might not lead to many sales.

With social media, you are typically paying for impressions and engagement. This means that you pay for the number of people who see your ad as well as for likes, comments, or any other type of engagement, regardless of whether anyone clicks and buys the book or not. This makes advertising on social media expensive.

Ad design

Another great thing with book platforms is that you don't need ad design. Amazon and Goodreads use your book cover and you only have to add text. On BookBub, you'll have the option of either using their simple and easy-to-use ad creator or upload your own ad.

Not having to deal with ad design will save you a lot of time, which is great, especially when you are already overburdened with other tasks. Successful writers can afford to hire designers who create great ads for them, but writers on a budget aren't quite there yet.

You'll need to invest every cent in ad distribution and newsletter promos first. Fancy ads won't be of much help if you don't have the money to show them to anyone.

Amazon Advertising

To get access to Amazon Advertising for books, you have to publish your book on Amazon KDP. You will see three dots next to your book In the Bookshelf on your KDP dashboard. Click them to open the options and select 'Promote and Advertise.'

This will give you several choices. You'll be able to enroll your book in KDP Select and get access to the promotion options that are only available to the books in KDP Select, and/or run a regular campaign using Amazon Advertising dashboard.

KDP Select

Not all writers agree on whether KDP Select is worth giving a try. Some authors in popular genres such as romance have had a huge success with it, while it didn't do much for others. How well this works seems to depend on the genre and author's popularity.

Just enrolling your ebook in KDP Select will not make it an overnight success, but it will lock it on Amazon for 90 days and during that time you won't be allowed to sell it anywhere else, including your website. This is not that great.

Two exclusive promotion options you will get if you decide to enroll your book in KDP select are Kindle Countdown Deal and Free Book Promotion. You cannot use both, so you'll have to choose either one or the other. This is not that great either.

With Kindle Countdown Deal, you can offer your book at a discount for 7 days. To be eligible for that, though, the regular price of the ebook has to be at least $2.99 and it must be enrolled in KDP Select for at least 30 days before you can start the promotion.

Another option is Free Book Promotion where you can offer your book for free for 5 days during a 90-day cycle of KDP Select enrollment. While this might have worked well in the past, it's questionable whether offering your book for free for five days would make much of a difference.

Whichever option you choose, you will also have to promote these deals to get some results And while KDP Select means that you may earn additional royalties from Kindle Unlimited and Kindle Owners' Lending Library, this might not lead to a significant increase in your earnings.

Regular ad campaigns

You can run ad campaigns on Amazon Advertising regardless of whether your book is enrolled in KDP Select or not. You have two options for ad placement – Sponsored Product and Product Display ads.

Most writers prefer Sponsored Product over Product Display but the only way to see what would work best for your book is to give both a try. You can place an unlimited number of ads and cancel them at any time, so don't be afraid to experiment.

Sponsored Product

Sponsored Product is an option Amazon recommends to beginners. Since many writers reported having more success with it than with Product Display, it might indeed be best to start with that.

You'll be able to choose between automatic and manual targeting. Automatic targeting means that Amazon's algorithm will find the best places for your book. With manual targeting, you will have to select keywords yourself.

Many authors recommend automatic targeting, but this really depends on the genre and type of the book. While automatic targeting works well for the most popular genres, it might not be as efficient for books that do not fit well into any genre.

With my book *The Story of the Fox and White Rabbit (not your ordinary fable)*, for instance, I got close to zero views with automatic, and thousands with manual targeting. On the other hand, though, automatic targeting worked better for this book.

Also, while non-fiction writers often recommend automatic targeting, fiction writers tend to prefer using book titles or names of successful writers who publish similar books in their genre. If you select automatic targeting, also keep in mind that you will have to let your ad run for a few weeks before Amazon's algorithm find the best placement for your book.

The minimal budget for Sponsored Product is $1 per day but you can safely go higher since you'll likely spend much less than the set budget. You can also set Sponsored Product campaigns to on-going with no end date.

Product Display

With Product Display ads, you'll be able to target either by product or by interest. Targeting by product may be useful if you want to place your book next to a popular book that has the same readers you are targeting.

Since popular books drive more traffic, having your book displayed next to it will lead to more exposure. Alternatively, you can also target based on the readers' interest, but this option only gives you a rather limited selection of the most popular genres.

Another interesting feature that might be useful in certain cases is the option to target products other than books. With Product Display, you can target any product on Amazon and not just books.

The minimal budget for Product Display campaign is $100. It's more than likely, though, that you won't come anywhere near spending that much, so don't be afraid to give it a try. Also, this type of campaigns can only be set for a limited duration and not as on-going.

Cost

Cost per click for both types of ads will depend on the category you choose, but is, in general, below a dollar per click. Since Amazon Advertising is getting more and more popular, however, the bids are rising. Try setting the bid a bit higher than the suggested bid if you aren't getting many impressions.

Targeting tips

Amazon will offer a list of keywords for your ad, but it's better to fine-tune these and replace them with your own selection. You can use Broad, Phrases, and Exact Match options. If you'd like to target only the readers who are looking for a specific book, use its title and select Phrase or Exact Match option.

If you are not sure which books by other writers you could use for targeting, try Yasiv [63]. Yasiv is a free online app that helps you find related books on Amazon. It shows you which books the readers who bought one book also bought. You can start by identifying the bestseller you'd like to use in your targeting and then check Yasiv to see which books these readers also bought.

The app is simple and easy to use. It presents the findings visually as a net of interconnected book covers and information about the books. When you access Yasiv, you will see only a search window, so don't let that confuse you. Put in the book title, author, or category and you will see the magic of Yasiv.

BookBub Partners

You'll have to create your author profile or Book Bub to get access to BookBub Partners platform. That's a great option for placing ads, for BookBub has millions of subscribers and getting your ad in front of so many readers is highly efficient.

On the downside, though, the platform is also highly competitive and if your ads don't have a good CTR, they will not be displayed very often. BookBub is all about best-sellers and that's why it has so many subscribers.

Ads by best-selling authors easily achieve CTR of over 1% or even over 4%. For an unknown writer, expecting to achieve that kind of CTR is a bit unrealistic. You'll thus have to keep coming up with different ads and try to achieve as high CTR as possible.

Cost

Bids on BookBub are relatively high and can easily exceed $1 per click. Most importantly, though, BookBub is where the readers are, so these ads might also convert better and lead to more sales.

Ad design

Unlike on Amazon and Goodreads, you can either upload your own ad or create one using the BookBub's simple ad creator. If you decide to design the ad yourself, I suggest you subscribe to their newsletter first to get an idea of how these ads look like and where they are placed. You will find them at the bottom of the newsletters.

Before you create an ad, also read the post "20 Top BookBub Ad Designs Readers Want to Click" with a selection of the most successful ads on BookBub [64]. You will see that quite a few of these ads were created using BookBub's ad creator so you really don't need any special ad design to get results. What matters more is the ad copy.

Targeting tips

A great thing about BookBub ads is the ability to target readers by country. You can do this by including the links to online stores in different countries, such as Amazon.au or Kobo.ca. You can thus send international readers straight to the platforms in their country.

BokBub will automatically pull in some of those links but you will have to manually add the ones that might be missing. Other than that, targeting on BookBub is quite limited and not best suited for all genres. You only have two options – to target by author or by category.

If you target by author, keep in mind that the only thing that counts here is the number of followers this author has on BookBub and nowhere else. You might thus choose a relatively popular author, but if they don't have a large following on BookBub, your ad will only be shown to a handful of subscribers.

As for targeting by category, there is only a basic list of genres, such as, 'General Nonfiction' or 'Supernatural Romance.' This is too limited when you need to target a more specific group of readers and even more so since you cannot add keywords or book titles. That's why it can be hard to achieve a good CTR on BookBub.

Goodreads

Goodreads is another platform created specifically for book lovers, which makes it a natural choice for book promotion. It, however, leaves much to be desired starting with a rather awkward user interface and limited targeting options. Still, Goodreads is a place where readers are, so you want to be there too. On the good note, ads on Goodreads are quite affordable.

Cost

The suggested bid on Goodreads is $0.50 but you can set it lower than that. Goodreads, however, is the only platform that uses a weird payment system where you have to pay in advance and then ask for a refund if you don't manage to spend the budget (which can happen). It's thus best to start with a small budget of $10 and then increase it if your ads are doing well.

Targeting tips

Targeting is another thing on Goodreads that could be better. You can, for instance, target by country but only by one at the time so that you have to create a new ad for each of the countries, which is tedious and time-consuming, to say the least.

You can target by genre. There, however, are not any additional targeting options available, such as by author, book title, or keywords. You also cannot target by age (even though Goodreads' advertising homepage claim you can) but you can target by gender, which may or might not be useful.

Social media advertising

A rather steep price is one of the issues with social media advertising. Another is that the users are accustomed to high-quality ads and you might not be able to come up with a good enough equivalent. It can thus be hard to get attention and convince people to check out your book.

Some authors highly recommend Facebook ads, but I cannot fully agree with them. For a writer on a budget, they might not always be the most cost-efficient option. You'll have to test different versions, create ad designs, find the right keywords, and try several approaches to achieve the results. That alone takes time and can be quite costly too.

It's also worth noting that many writers who have had success with social media ads promote one book in a series rather than a stand-alone book. Promoting a book in a series leads to more sales of the other books too, which makes this option financially viable.

For all these reasons, I suggest you don't place all the bets on social media paid ads as the main driving force of your campaign, and even less so if you're only starting out and have published one book.

Also, not all social media advertising platforms are worth giving a try. Ads on Twitter, for instance, became more expensive than ads on Facebook and Instagram. The last time I tried it, I had to pay $5 for two clicks and paying that much makes no sense whatsoever.

Marketing expert Larry Kim has been monitoring and comparing Twitter and Facebook ads. In his latest 2018 update, he stated that you are better off with Facebook on almost every level. In his opinion, Facebook ads work best for big brands and content marketing – providing you can afford them [65].

Facebook can indeed be great for driving paid traffic to blog posts. That's how you can get sales by creating a good content, and that's an example of recommended use. Creating and placing image or video ads on Facebook, however, is another story. You'd need to invest a lot more and this will likely not be cost-efficient for a beginner.

The thing is, it's far from easy to master social media advertising. Facebook's advertising dashboard is a complex tool and it takes a while before you learn how to use it. For good results, you need to figure out what kind of ad would work best for your book, know how to target well, where to place ads, and how to select the right objectives.

Creating a good ad is a challenge but that's just the beginning. Running an ad campaign on Facebook is on a higher intermediate level, and since this is a book for beginners, I will only introduce you to the simplest and easiest options that can bring results.

Facebook & Instagram

To start promoting, you'll first need to create a business page on Facebook. If you want to promote on Instagram too, you'll need to create a business account there as well and then connect the two. You can advertise on both platforms through Facebook's advertising dashboard that gives you a variety of different advertising options. You can:

- Boost posts
- Create offers
- Place paid ads (image, video, stories)
- Get more page likes

The easiest of these to set up are post boosts, offers, and page likes. I, however, do not recommend paying for page likes since that won't make any difference in the visibility of the posts on your business page.

Post boosts

This is the simplest and easiest promotion option and thus recommended for beginners. When you publish a post on your Facebook business page, you will see a 'Boost Post' button at the bottom of the post.

You can use that to promote a post to an audience you select. This option is perfect when you publish a helpful post or interesting story related to your non-fiction of fiction book. It doesn't look like an annoying ad and is in line with what people like to see on social media – interesting and useful content.

You can then promote your book in the blog post rather than directly on Facebook or Instagram. This option is also great because you don't have to waste time on designing ads and trying to come up with a good ad copy. Instead, you just link the blog post and promote that.

Besides, the average CTR for ads on Facebook is only 0.119% [65]. Good content, on the other hand, converts much better and you can get a lot more from boosting an interesting blog post than from trying to impress with an ad.

Offers

You can also create offers as a type of post on your business page. This can be useful when you are running a free book promotion campaign or offering your book at a discount. You, can, for instance, use an offer to promote a special preorder price or a Kindle Countdown Deal.

Creating an offer is easy. Start creating a new post on your business page and select 'Offer' among the options on the top of the post. After you publish the offer, use the Boost Post option to promote it.

Audience

When you boost a post, you'll be able to create and save an audience. You will be able to customize your audience by gender, age, location (down to the postal code), and interests.

Facebook will automatically suggest interests based on your keywords, which makes boosting posts quite easy. Things, however, get a lot more complicated when you try to create an ad.

To do that, click 'Create' in the top Facebook menu and select "Ad.' This will take you to Facebook's advertising dashboard where you'll have to choose among 11 available marketing objectives to begin with. You'll be able to set up an A/B campaign, bidding strategy, and play with numerous additional options.

While this is great for marketing savvy people, it can be overwhelming for someone who's faced with these options and terminology for the first time in their lives.

Paid ads

If you nevertheless decide to give paid ads a try, it might be best to use video instead of image ads. Video ads are growing in popularity and have a higher CTR than image ads [66]. You, however, will need a great video that is on par with the level of quality social media users expect.

You can create different types of ads on Instagram – photo, video, carousel, and stories. Instagram has excellent support pages that explain these options and what you can do with them quite well. As the platform's popularity skyrocketed, though, so did the cost.

Running a promotion on Instagram is now more expensive than on Facebook. If you cannot afford ads of comparable quality and the high price of advertising, placing ads on Instagram might not be best and certainly not the most affordable option.

Placement

Regardless of which type of promotion you choose, be careful with the placement and avoid Facebook's default 'Automatic placement' option. When you boost a post, you'll find that option just below the 'Audience.'

Turn it off, so that you will be able to manually choose the best placement options for your ad. The three basic options in boosted posts are Facebook, Messenger, and Instagram. You'll have more options in the Ad Manager dashboard.

Instagram can be very expensive, so you might want to turn that off if your budget is low. Also, make sure to check how the ad looks like in each of the placement options – you will see the mockups displayed next to them. Not every placement will be a good fit for every post or ad, so remove those that don't work well.

Cost control

Another thing that you have to take care of is cost control. This will, again, be quite easy to set up with the post-boost option, and more complicated when you create ads in Facebook's advertising dashboard.

When you boost a post, you'll be able to set the budget and duration of the campaign so there will be no surprises. If you are placing ads, though, I suggest you set up the spending limit in the Payment Settings because the cost can build up pretty fast.

29. AD DESIGN & COPY TIPS

While you can avoid designing ads for most promotion channels, you will nevertheless need to present and promote your books on your website. You could use a simple 2D book cover for the purpose, but the book will look so much better if you use 3D book mockups instead.

3D book mockups

3D mockups can make all the difference in how the readers perceive your book and you as an author. Some writers get mockups at an affordable price on Fiverr. If you a writer on a budget, however, you might want to save every cent and do as much as you can yourself.

Luckily, it's not that hard to create a mockup. There are free online apps that let you create basic 3D mockups on a white background. For more complex options, though, you'll need access to Photoshop or use an open source program GIMP.

Covervault

Covervault is a great option for elegant and professional looking 3D book mockups that include background images [67]. It offers a wide selection of different backgrounds and book sizes as well as paperback, hardcover, and mobile editions.

If you have Photoshop, it will be very easy to use these mockups. Covervault's has a video tutorial with step-by-step instructions. You can also use GIMP since it's open source program and thus free to use. GIMP, however, doesn't support smart objects, which is what these mockups are based on, so you'll have to replace the images manually.

DIY Book Cover

DIY Book Covers' 3D mockup generator is another option that is even easier to use [68]. It only creates mockups on a white background, though, but you can use the app online and create a mockup in seconds.

You can also pick either a single book or a combination of different book editions. Make a choice, upload your book cover, and download the mockup – it's that simple. There is no faster and easier option than DIY Book Covers.

BoxShot Lite

Another option is BoxShot Lite – a free 3D book cover maker [69]. This option is also available as an online app. Its use, however, is limited to a single 3D paperback image on a white background.

There is one feature, though, that separates BoxShot from the rest and makes it an interesting option. You can play with the position of the book as much as you like and even adjust the shadow. This lets you create something quite unique that has a less generic feel to it.

Ad copy tips

When writing a copy for your ad, remember that book description and ad copy are not one and the same thing. Ad copy is one of the hardest forms of writing since you need to hook the reader with a single short sentence.

Try to put yourself in the shoes of the person who will see your ad. What, apart from the image, would make them notice and pay attention to it? What kind of ads do you notice and why? Remember, you only have a split second to get their attention.

State the benefits

With how-to books, you are offering a solution to a certain problem the reader is struggling with. With memoir, you are letting the reader peek in the most private parts of your life so that they can experience something special they never would have been able to if it weren't for your story.

Fiction can satisfy a wide range of needs – a desire for love and romance, the excitement of an adventure while staying in the safety of one's home, an escape from a gruesome everyday reality if only for a few hours, or life-changing views that have the power to shatter and change the reader's perspective…

Whatever your story, you need to make it clear what's in it for the reader. This will be easier for how-to books, but for fiction, you need to know what kind of desire or need the book fulfills and base your ad copy on that.

Additional benefits you can also use in the ad are the price or any special achievements, such as the best-selling rank. If you are running a free book promotion or offer your book at a discount, make sure to point that out too.

Study best practices and run tests

Go through the selection of previously mentioned best performing ads on BookBub [64] and check the ads. You will see that they all have one thing in common – they make the benefit of reading the book clear.

Also, test different versions of your ad to see which one works best. The results can be surprising since no one can predict with absolute certainty which copy will convert better [70]. That's why A/B tests are routinely used in professional marketing.

30. GIVEAWAYS

Setting priorities can be hard since we would all like to do as much as we can. With self-publishing on a budget, however, there are limits to what we can afford, and giveaways might thus be one of the things that will just have to wait.

While there are cheap or even free giveaway options available, for instance, on Amazon, they come with far too few useful features to be worth the effort. It's also questionable how well offering your book as a prize will work if you don't have a following yet.

Amazon

You can set up a giveaway on Amazon.com for free by scrolling all the way down on the book product page. You'll find 'Set up a giveaway' button there. If you are not from the States, you might only be able to use this option for print editions, though.

This can make giveaways on Amazon quite costly for international writers since you'll have to cover the cost of shipping in addition to the price of the book. It's also questionable what could you achieve by running a giveaway on Amazon.

The main problem with these giveaways is that you can only ask for one thing as an entry requirement and there are only three options you can choose from: those who enter would have to either follow you on Amazon, watch a Video Short, or watch a YouTube video. None of this is useful since what you need are the participants' emails, and you won't get these on Amazon.

Goodreads

You can also set up a giveaway on Goodreads. The price, however, is rather steep - $119 for Standard and $599 for Premium package. You'll have to pay this regardless of the number of entries and success of your giveaways. If you are promoting on a budget, there are better ways of spending that much money.

Giveaway services

Some writers offer best-sellers by other writers in their genre as a prize. They use this approach to build an email list in hope of selling their books to these subscribers later on [71]. For that, however, you have to use a giveaway service, such as KingSumo, Book Funnel, or Gleam.

These services, however, can be quite costly and you'll also have to promote the giveaway if you want it to succeed. This can quickly add up to several hundred dollars, which is what a writer on a budget usually have available for the whole campaign rather than a single giveaway.

31. OTHER OPTIONS

What we have explored so far are the basic promotion options you should be familiar with. This, however, doesn't mean that's all there is to it. There are many other possibilities and you can always come up with new ideas – the more creative, the better.

Basically, it all comes down to time and money. Most of the additional options listed in this chapter will add to your expenses. Production of video trailers, audiobooks, and online course, for instance, can be expensive unless you know how to do it yourself and have the right equipment.

The option that doesn't cost anything is merchandise, but you'll have to choose the products, prepare the designs, and find the right platform and print-on-demand (POD) service for selling them.

These might thus not the best options for a beginner on a budget who doesn't have much time on their hands. At some point in the future, though, you might be able to use them and grow your self-publishing business.

Video trailers

If you can do it yourself or can afford to hire someone to do it for you, producing a video trailer is a good idea. You can use it as an ad, on your website, upload it to YouTube, and add it to your author page on Amazon. The popularity of video ads and book trailers is on the rise, so you should consider this option at some point in the future.

Audiobooks

Audiobooks are an interesting option too. They can add to the royalties and offer a fresh opportunity for promotion of a new edition of your book. You can also reach a new audience through this channel. Like video trailers, though, producing an audiobook is expensive unless you can do it yourself and have the right equipment for that too.

Online Courses

Many writers, especially those who publish non-fiction, don't just sell books but also offer additional services related to the book. Among the popular options are online courses and webinars. If you are comfortable in front of the camera and have a knack for teaching, this might be a good option that can bring in additional income. You can also promote your book to those who take the course.

Merchandise

In music, film, and publishing industry, selling all sorts of products in addition to the main one (in our case, a book) is an established practice. You can sell apparel, coffee mugs, prints, and other items using images or quotes from your books.

The best part of this is that you don't have to invest anything, since there are many POD services you can use. You will only have to come up with the designs and learn how to prepare them for print. If you are going to use the artwork created for your book, though, make sure you have the rights to use it for this purpose too.

32. PROMOTION PLAN

Now that you are familiar with both free and paid promotion options and have a better understanding of the costs and risks, it's time to prepare a strategy and promotion plan for your book.

As you've probably realized by now, the results of book promotion can be unpredictable. They will depend on many factors and some of these might be beyond your control. You can do everything right, but if, for instance, other writers heavily promote competing titles at the time of your launch, this can have a negative effect on your sales.

While it is good to have a plan, it is thus also advisable to remain flexible and be prepared to make changes if needed. But your strategy and promotion plan will above all depend on the available budget.

Plan activities by cost

When you start planning your campaign, go through the list of available options and then make the final selection and plan based on the available time and budget:

- Blogging
- Guest blogging and publishing in publications
- Newsletters and social media
- Paid ads on book promotion sites
- Paid ads on book platforms
- Paid ads on social media

- Free books and giveaways

Start by making a list of blog posts or stories you will publish on your blog. Then make a list of guest blog options or publications you could pitch or submit your stories to. You'll have to plan these pitches in advance since having a guest post published takes time.

Include news about the book in the newsletters to your subscribers. Ideally, you would start sharing these weeks or even months before you publish the book. Use social media to keep your followers posted too. These activities cost nothing but can be highly efficient.

You can experiment with boosting your blog posts on social media to see how many visitors that brings to your blog and if it leads to new subscribers and sales.

Next, plan promotion on book promotion sites based on your budget. Make a selection of the best and most affordable sites and check their book policy as well as available dates. Start working on that well before your desired promotion dates since the best sites can be booked for weeks in advance.

Allocate the remaining budget to Amazon Advertising, Goodreads, and BookBub and set up the ads there too. If you can afford it, create a video book trailer and upload it to your website, YouTube, and author page on Amazon as well as promote it on social media.

Plan long-term

If you want your book to rank higher on Amazon, it's much better to have the sales spread across a longer period than squashed in a day or two. Your book's rank will improve if it consistently sells a few copies a day rather than get many sales in one day followed by weeks of inactivity. Plan your campaign based on the following phases and create a timeline for the promotion activities:

- Pre-launch
- Launch
- Second push
- On-going promotion

Pre-launch

Start building awareness while you are still working on the book. Spread the news about it through your blog, social media, newsletter, and stories in publications. You can also publish excerpts from the book. Use all channels, including your email signature, to let your audience know about the new book.

If you offer your book for preorder, you can also start using paid promotion options to get as many sales as possible before the publishing date. Since the book doesn't have reviews while available for preorder, set the price low and promote it at a special preorder price.

Launch

If you ran a preorder, you can raise the price after the book gets published and you already got the first reviews. Rather err on the side of setting the price too low than too high, though. If you launched without a preorder, start with the lowest price and keep it low until you get reviews and a decent number of sales. You need to promote your book heavily during this time.

Second push

Plan for your second push based on the results you've achieved during the pre-launch and launch. If the results weren't great, consider the buyer's journey and take the time to troubleshoot and fix anything that could negatively affect the sales – book cover, blurb, ad copy, etc.

If everything went well, you can offer your book for free for a limited time and use that for the second promotion boost. After that, you will ideally be able to start selling the book at a higher price.

On-going promotion

Use the on-going campaign option on Amazon, Goodreads, or Book Bub ads – the platforms that let you promote regardless of the book's price. Don't forget to keep building your platform and growing your following by consistently publishing blog posts and stories. This too as a form of an on-going promotion.

33. USEFUL APPS AND TOOLS

Here is a list of useful apps and tools that can help you get things done faster at no or low cost. I already mentioned some of these in the book. In this chapter, however, I added additional ones and placed them in categories, so that you can easily find what you need.

Social media management

Buffer

Buffer [72] allows you to schedule and share your posts to several social media at once. The basic free plan lets you schedule 10 posts in advance and share them to up to three social media accounts.

Gramblr

Gramblr [73] is an app that lets you post on Instagram from your PC instead of a mobile device. It includes a basic image editor too.

Linktr.ee

Linktree [8] lets you create a menu with different links which you can share on a single URL. This is perfect for Instagram and other social media profiles.

Design and 3D mockups

Creative Market

You can find a wide array of design resources, such as templates, fonts, and Photoshop tools on Creative Market [74]. If you subscribe to the newsletter, you will receive 6 free resources every week.

Snappa and Canva

Snappa [75] and Canva [76] are online design apps you can use to create ads, book covers, and social media images. The apps include a selection of premade templates, free pictures, and fonts.

GIMP

GIMP [33] is a free alternative to Photoshop. It takes a bit of learning but there are numerous free tutorials available online.

Covervault

Covervault [67] offers a range of free 3D book mockups that include background images. You'll have to replace the book cover image yourself and will need Photoshop for full functionality. You can use GIMP and get decent results as well, but it will take more work.

DIY Book Cover

DIY Book Cover [68] is another free app you can use to create ebook and print book 3D mockups. Numerous templates with different combinations of editions are available (ebooks, mobile devices, print editions).

BoxShot Lite

BoxShot Lite [69] is also a free 3D book mockup app. This is a less generic option since you can freely set up the book's position in a 3D environment.

Google Fonts

Google Fonts [77] is a library of 900 free fonts you can upload to your computer and use in your designs.

Free images and videos

Stock Up

Stock Up [78] collects free high-quality images from several stock photo sites. Check the image licenses to see whether they include modification of the image and give proper attribution when required.

Unsplash

Unsplash [79] offers a wide selection of free photos and is inbuilt in Medium. If you blog on Medium, click the plus sign in the draft of your post and then select search icon (not photo icon) to get direct access to Unsplash.

Pixabay

In addition to photos, you can find free videos, vector graphics, and illustrations on Pixabay [80].

Topic finders and title generators

Title Generators

Kindlepreneur prepared a great selection of title and content idea generators [81].

Quora

Subscribe to Quora's newsletter [82], and you will never run out of ideas. You will also discover that life can indeed be weirder than fiction.

Keywords and Amazon categories

Kindle Ranker

Kindle Ranker [39] is an affordable alternative to K-lytics and KDP Rocket. It helps you find the best categories for your book using a range of useful parameters. You get two free queries per day.

Yasiv

Yasiv [63] helps you select keywords when you target by book titles and authors. It shows you the books that were also bought by the readers who purchased these books.

Book sales analytics

Book Report

Book Report app [83] gives you an overview of your books' sales, reviews, and rank on Amazon.

Website tools

Website Grader

If you have a website, regularly check for any SEO issue that might negatively affect your site's ranking on Google. Website Grader [84] will create a quick report, including suggestions for improvements.

TinyPNG

If you use too many or too large images on your website, this can be a problem. Check the images with TinyPNG image analyzer [85] and then use TinyPNG to compress them if needed.

Broken link checkup

Broken links can have a negative effect on website ranking too. Broken Link Checkup [86] is a free tool you can use to make sure there aren't any on your website.

Add This

Add This [22] offers a range of free website tools, such as social buttons and fancy signup forms. You'll need to know how to use HTML code to use it, though.

Social media ads

Facebook Ads Grader

Free Facebook Ads Grader [87] will evaluate your Facebook ads and prepare a report with suggestions for improvement.

34. FINAL WORD

Mastering book promotion takes time. There is a lot to take in and it's easy to feel overwhelmed, especially when you are doing this for the first time. My advice would thus be to:

- Take it one step at the time
- Know that failing is a part of the process
- Learn and keep learning.

Check the Recommended Reading on the next page too, there is a lot of useful information there. You can also visit my website (matejaklaric.com) and subscribe for my monthly newsletter where I share the news and report on my self-publishing journey.

Just like you, I am a writer on a budget. I have to find ways to promote my books with minimal funds while competing with writers who can spend in a day what I have available for the whole campaign. That's why I'm writing this *Self-Publishing Made Easy* series in hope that it will be of help to you too.

Finally, remember how important reviews are? Please consider leaving one for this book. Thank you!

Recommended reading

"Top Ten Publishing Trends Every Author Needs to Know In 2018". Ricci - Written Word Media, 2018. https://www.writtenwordmedia.com/2018/01/08/publishing-trends-indie-publishing/

"Sending Ham, Not Spam: Using Email Best Practices for A Better Campaign - Email Marketing Tips". Hollis, Sam - Email Marketing Tips, 2018. https://blog.aweber.com/articles-tips/sending-ham-not-spam-using-email-best-practices-for-a-better-campaign.htm

"Should Marketers Use Pop-Up Forms? A Comprehensive Analysis". Ratner, Ben – Hubspot Blog, 2018. https://blog.hubspot.com/marketing/pop-up-forms-analysis

"Book Cover Design Prices In 2018 - Rocking Book Covers". Adrijus - Rocking Book Covers, 2018. https://www.rockingbookcovers.com/book-cover-design/book-cover-design-prices-2017/

"How to Write A Blurb - Definition, Examples, And More". Blurb Blog, 2018. http://www.blurb.com/blog/writing-blurbs-for-novels/

"Writing A Killer Logline Using the Killogator Logline Formula". Graeme Shimmin, Spy Thriller and Alternate History Writer, 2018. http://graemeshimmin.com/writing-a-logline-for-a-novel/

"Book Cover Taglines: Make It Snappy". Dearsley, K.S. - Wow-Womenonwriting.Com, 2018. http://www.wow-womenonwriting.com/69-FE-Taglines.HTML

"Optimizing Your Books for Amazon Keyword Search". Sansevieri, Penny - Jane Friedman, 2018. https://www.janefriedman.com/optimizing-books-amazon-keyword-search/

"Are Paid Book Reviews Worth It?". Jane Friedman, 2018. https://www.janefriedman.com/paid-book-reviews/

"How to Set Up a Draft2Digital Author Page". Ferguson, Jamie - Blackbird Publishing, 2018. https://blackbirdpublishing.com/how-to-set-up-a-draft2digital-author-page/

"One Author's Experience With 19 Promo Sites". Heffernan, Laura - Writer Unboxed, 2018. https://writerunboxed.com/2017/09/03/do-daily-deal-services-work-one-authors-experience-with-18-promo-sites/

"20 Top BookBub Ad Designs Readers Want to Click". Urban, Diana - BookBub Partners Blog, 2018. https://insights.bookbub.com/top-bookbub-ad-designs-readers-want-to-click/

"Facebook Video Ads: 15 Essential Best Practices For 2018". Gollin, Maxwell - Falcon.Io, 2018. https://www.falcon.io/insights-hub/topics/social-media-strategy/facebook-video-ads-best-practices-for-2018/

"Why Instagram Video Ads May Be A Good Fit for Your Brand". Vrountas, Ted - Instapage.Com, 2018.
https://instapage.com/blog/instagram-video-ads

"The Book P&L: How Publishers Make Decisions About What to Publish". Jane Friedman, 2018.
https://www.janefriedman.com/book-pl/

"Best and Worst Self-Publishing Services Rated by The Alliance of Independent Authors". Alliance of Independent Authors: Self-Publishing Advice Center, 2018.
https://selfpublishingadvice.org/allis-self-publishing-service-directory/self-publishing-service-reviews/

"Book Publishing Has a Data Problem, and the Industry Is Finding Solutions". What's New In Publishing, 2018.
https://whatsnewinpublishing.com/2018/09/book-publishing-has-a-data-problem-and-the-industry-is-finding-solutions/

References

1

"How the Rule Of 7 Can Radically Grow Your Business". Stevens, John - The Balance Small Business, 2018. https://www.thebalancesmb.com/how-to-use-the-rule-of-7-to-radically-grow-your-business-4037683

2

"Amazon.com Help: Profile & Community Guidelines". Amazon.com, 2018. https://www.amazon.com/gp/help/customer/display.HTML?nodeId=201929730

3

"AUTHOR ALERT! How Amazon Can Instantly (Poof!) Make Your Book Sales DISAPPEAR!". Hoy, Angela – WritersWeekly.com, 2018. https://writersweekly.com/angela-desk/how-amazon-can-kill-your-book-sales

4

"Genre Guide". Written Word Media, 2018. https://secure.writtenwordmedia.com/genre-guide

5

"A Leaderboard for Medium Publications - Top Medium Publications". Top Pub, 2018. https://toppub.xyz/publications

6

"SPF Blog Post Submission". Self-Publishing Formula, 2018. https://selfpublishingformula.com/guest-post-submission/

7

"2017 Smashwords Survey of Ebook Trends and Data". Slideshare, 2017. https://www.slideshare.net/Smashwords/2017-smashwords-survey-of-ebook-trends-and-data

8

"Linktree". Linktree, 2018. https://linktr.ee/

9

"Jay Kristoff (@Misterkristoff)". Instagram, 2018. https://www.instagram.com/misterkristoff/

10

"Victoria Schwab (@Veschwab)". Instagram, 2018. https://www.instagram.com/veschwab/

11

"Getting Started on Instagram for Businesses". Instagram For Business, 2018.
https://business.instagram.com/getting-started

12

"How to Set Up Shopping on Instagram". Instagram For Business, 2018.
https://business.instagram.com/a/shopping-setup-guide

13

"Facebook vs Twitter Advertising: Where Should You Invest?". Brisk, Simon – Jeff Bullas' Blog, 2018.
https://www.jeffbullas.com/facebook-vs-twitter-advertising-invest/

14

"Reddit Is the Third-Most-Popular Destination on the Internet". Nguyen, Chuong - Digital Trends, 2018.
https://www.digitaltrends.com/computing/reddit-more-popular-than-facebook-in-2018/

15

"Nosleep". Reddit, 2018. https://www.reddit.com/r/nosleep

16

"Short Stories". Reddit, 2018.
https://www.reddit.com/r/shortstories/

17

"Reddit — One of The World's Most Popular Websites — Is Trying to Cash In Through Advertising". Castillo, Michelle - CNBC, 2018. https://www.cnbc.com/2018/06/29/how-reddit-plans-to-make-money-through-advertising.HTML

18

"Email Signup Benchmarks: How Many Visitors Should Be Converting". Peterson, Sarah - Sumo, 2018.
https://sumo.com/stories/email-signup-benchmarks

19

"Embeddable Newsletter Signup Forms". Upscri.be, 2018.
https://upscri.be/

20

"Newsletter Plugins". Wordpress.org, 2018.
https://wordpress.org/plugins/search/newsletter/

21

"Are Email Subscription Pop-Ups Worth the Risk?". Andrea, Mauro D. - Unbounce, 2012. https://unbounce.com/email-marketing/get-subscribers-from-pop-ups/

22

"Free Website Tools". AddThis, 2018. https://www.addthis.com/

23

"How Can I Set an Expiration for a Shared Link?". Dropbox.Com, 2018. https://www.dropbox.com/help/files-folders/link-expiration

24

"Amazon Purchase of Goodreads Stuns Book Industry". Flood, Alison - The Guardian, 2013. https://www.theguardian.com/books/2013/apr/02/amazon-purchase-goodreads-stuns-book-industry

25

"Mateja Klaric Author Page". Books2read.Com, 2018. https://www.books2read.com/ap/nOLLz8/Mateja-Klaric

26

"Lifeinlit (@Lifeinlit)". Instagram, 2018.
https://www.instagram.com/lifeinlit/

27

"Branding & Corporate Identity – Learn". Learn, 2018.
https://www.canva.com/learn/branding-identity-design/

28

"The Top 12 Advanced SEO Tips Every Blogger Should Know". Barrington, Katherine – SEO SiteCheckup, 2018.
https://seositecheckup.com/articles/the-top-12-advanced-seo-tips-every-blogger-should-know

29

"New Book P&L". Berrett-Koehler Publishers. Slideshare, 2012.
https://www.slideshare.net/davidpaulmarshall/berrettkoehler-publishers-new-book-pl

30

"Book Cover Design Prices In 2018". Adrijus - Rocking Book Covers, 2018.
https://www.rockingbookcovers.com/book-cover-design/book-cover-design-prices-2017/

31

"Premade Book Covers". The Book Cover Designer, 2018. https://thebookcoverdesigner.com/

32

"Premade Book Covers by Mariah Sinclair". The Cover Vault, 2018. https://thecovervault.com/

33

"GIMP - GNU Image Manipulation Program". GIMP, 2018. https://www.gimp.org/

34

"How to Write A Blurb - Definition, Examples, And More". Blurb Blog, 2018. http://www.blurb.com/blog/writing-blurbs-for-novels/

35

"Cottage by The Sea by Debbie Macomber". Penguin Random House, 2018. https://www.penguinrandomhouse.com/books/553678/cottage-by-the-sea-by-debbie-macomber/

36

"Clear and Present Danger (Movie Tie-In) by Tom Clancy". Penguin Random House, 2018.

https://www.penguinrandomhouse.com/books/291932/clear-and-present-danger-movie-tie-in-by-tom-clancy/9780440001065

37

"20 Top Bookbub Ad Designs Readers Want to Click". Urban, Diana - Bookbub Partners Blog, 2018. https://insights.bookbub.com/top-bookbub-ad-designs-readers-want-to-click/

38

"Ebook Pricing Strategies to Sell More Books and Maximize Author Earnings". Chloe - Written Word Media, 2018. https://www.writtenwordmedia.com/2018/07/25/ebook-pricing/

39

"Find the Best Amazon Book Categories". Kindle Ranker, 2018. https://www.kindleranker.com/

40

"Are Paid Book Reviews Worth It?". Jane Friedman, 2016. https://www.janefriedman.com/paid-book-reviews/

41

"Don't Throw Out the Baby! Why #Amazon Doesn't Want Your #Bookreviews". Barb Taub, 2018.

https://barbtaub.com/2018/04/15/dont-throw-out-the-baby-why-amazon-doesnt-want-your-bookreviews/

42

"Book Reviews". The Kindle Book Review, 2018. https://www.thekindlebookreview.net/book-reviews/

43

"Profile & Community Guidelines". Amazon.com, 2018. https://www.amazon.com/gp/help/customer/display.HTML?nodeId=14279631

44

"The Best Book Blogs That do Free Book Reviews". Booksirens, 2018. https://booksirens.com/book-reviewer-directory

45

"The Best Book Review Blogs In 2018". Reedsy, 2018. https://blog.reedsy.com/book-review-blogs/

46

"Booktube Channel Guide • A Curated List Of 100+ Booktubers". Reedsy, 2018. https://blog.reedsy.com/booktube-channels/

47

"Mark Dawson Shares His Secret Facebook Ads Strategy". Reedsy, 2015. https://blog.reedsy.com/facebook-ads-for-authors-mark-dawson-interview/

48

"Writing 50,000 Words With 10 Other Writers -- In A Castle". Pequenino, Karla - CNN, 2016. https://edition.cnn.com/2016/11/21/world/french-writers-castle-trnd/index.HTML

49

"Meredith Wild, A Self-Publisher Making an Imprint". Alter, Alexandra - The New York Times, 2016. https://www.nytimes.com/2016/01/31/business/media/meredith-wild-a-self-publisher-making-an-imprint.HTML

50

"The Book P&L: How Publishers Make Decisions About What to Publish". Jane Friedman, 2015. https://www.janefriedman.com/book-pl/

51

"How to Self-Publish Your Book: The Fast, Free & Easy Way". Klaric, Mateja - Books2Read, 2018. https://www.books2read.com/self-publish-second-edition

52

"Survey Indicates Indie Publishing is Pot of Gold for Some, Work in Progress for Many". Force, Marie and Serra, Cheryl - Marie Force Blog, 2016.
https://blog.marieforce.com/survey-indicates-indie-publishing-is-pot-of-gold-for-some-work-in-progress-for-many/

53

"Analytics Tools & Solutions for Your Business - Google Analytics". Google Marketing Platform, 2018.
https://marketingplatform.google.com/about/analytics/

54

"How Many Amazon Kindle Ebooks are There in The Kindle Store?". Haines, Derek - Just Publishing Advice, 2018.
https://justpublishingadvice.com/how-many-kindle-ebooks-are-there/

55

"Return on Investment (ROI) Calculator". Calculator, 2018.
https://www.calculator.net/roi-calculator.HTML

56

"Book Promotion Services 2018: The Best Free and Paid Promo Services". Reedsy Tools, 2018.
https://blog.reedsy.com/book-promotion-services/

57

"Best and Worst Self-Publishing Services Rated by The Alliance of Independent Authors". Alliance of Independent Authors: Self-Publishing Advice Center, 2018. https://selfpublishingadvice.org/allis-self-publishing-service-directory/self-publishing-service-reviews/

58

"Bookbub Partners". BookBub, 2018. https://partners.bookbub.com/

59

"The BookBub Partners Blog | Book Marketing & Publishing Tips". BookBub Partners Blog, 2018. https://insights.bookbub.com/

60

"Ebook Hounds Pricing". Ebook Hounds, 2018. https://www.ebookhounds.com/pricing/

61

"Genre Pulse – Kindle Book Promotion". genre pulse, 2018. http://www.genrepulse.com/

62

"Stats – Genre Pulse". genre pulse, 2018. http://www.genrepulse.com/stats/

63

"Amazon Products Visualization - YASIV". Kashcha, Andrei - Yasiv, 2018. http://yasiv.com/

64

"20 Top BookBub Ad Designs Readers Want to Click". Urban, Diana - BookBub Partners Blog, 2018. https://insights.bookbub.com/top-bookbub-ad-designs-readers-want-to-click/

65

"Do Twitter Ads Work? Comparing the Ad Performance of The World's Largest Social Networks". Kim, Larry - WordStream, 2018. https://www.wordstream.com/blog/ws/2013/11/05/twitter-versus-facebook-ad-performance

66

"Video Ads vs. Traditional Banners - Measuring Effectiveness". Robertson, Mark R. - Tubular Insights, 2018. https://tubularinsights.com/video-ads-more-effective/

67

"Free PSD Mockups for Books and More!". Covervault, 2018. https://covervault.com/

68

"The 3D Book Cover Creator You'll Love to Use". DIY Book Covers, 2018. https://diybookcovers.com/3Dmockups/

69

"Make 3D Book Covers Online for Free". BoxShot Lite, 2018. https://boxshot.com/3d-pack/3d-book/

70

"How to Write Attention-Grabbing Promo Copy for Books [Book Marketing 101]". Rose, M. J. - BookBub Partners Blog, 2018. https://insights.bookbub.com/write-attention-grabbing-promo-copy-books/

71

"6 Steps for Building Your Author Mailing List Through Giveaways". Reedsy, 2015. https://blog.reedsy.com/6-steps-for-building-your-author-mailing-list-through-giveaways/

72

"Buffer - A Smarter Way to Share on Social Media". Buffer, 2018. https://buffer.com/app

73

"Gramblr - Upload Photos to Instagram From Your PC, Mac, Computer!". Gramblr, 2018. https://gramblr.com/uploader/#home

74

"Fonts, Graphics, Themes, and More". Creative Market, 2018. https://creativemarket.com/

75

"Snappa - Create Online Graphics in a Snap". Snappa, 2018. https://snappa.com/

76

"Amazingly Simple Graphic Design Software – Canva". Canva, 2018. https://www.canva.com/

77

"Google Fonts". Google Fonts, 2018. https://fonts.google.com/

78

"Searching 25,000+ Free Stock Photos". Stock Up, 2018. https://www.sitebuilderreport.com/stock-up

79

"Beautiful Free Images & Pictures". Unsplash, 2018. https://unsplash.com/

80

"Stunning Free Images". Pixabay, 2018. https://pixabay.com/

81

"Book Title Generators: List of the Best Free Book Name Generators". Kindlepreneur, 2018. https://kindlepreneur.com/free-book-title-generator-tools/

82

"Question and Answer Website". Quora, 2018. https://www.quora.com/

83

"Book Report", 2018. https://app.getbookreport.com/

84

"Website Grader". HubSpot, Inc., 2018.
https://website.grader.com/

85

"Web Page Image Analyzer". TinyPNG, 2018.
https://tinypng.com/analyzer

86

"Free Broken Link Checker - Online Dead Link Checking Tool". Broken Link Checker, 2018.
https://www.brokenlinkcheck.com/

87

"Facebook Ads Performance Grader". WordStream, 2018.
https://www.wordstream.com/facebook-advertising

About the author

Mateja started to write short stories at the age of ten and later became a freelance journalist, radio personality, and explorer of the inner worlds. To make life even more fun, she also ran an advertising agency for eight years. Apart from that, Mateja's life resembles a roller coaster ride full of ups and downs and some pretty wild turns. Among other things, her car was destroyed by tanks, and she survived several brushes with death. Mateja graduated in psychology from Arizona State University and is now a writer, photographer, and transformational guide.

matejaklaric.com

Also by Mateja Klaric

Self-Publishing Made Easy, Book 1
How to Self-Publish Your Book: The Fast, Free & Easy Way
2nd Edition (2018)

A step-by-step guide to the technical aspects of self-publishing for absolute beginners. It will teach you how to format your book in MS Word, prepare and format images for print, design your book cover using free tools, and more. You will get a general overview of everything you need to self-publish your first book the fast, free, and easy way.

The Fox & White Rabbit, Book 1
The Story of the Fox and White Rabbit
(not your ordinary fable)

The fox leads a cruel and merciless life until one night in the woods changes everything. A chance meeting with magical White Rabbit leaves the fox shaken to the core. Nothing will ever be the same again.

www.ingramcontent.com/pod-product-compliance
Lightning Source LLC
Chambersburg PA
CBHW071537220526
45469CB00003B/812